Praise for *Rebel*

"If you've ever felt stuck, frustrated, or disappointed by how life has turned out so far, this book will give you the clarity, confidence, and inspiration to live your one precious life authentically and uniquely to the fullest."

—Jon Gordon, fifteen-time Bestselling Author, *The Energy Bus* and *The One Truth*

"My favorite thing about Graham is that he lives what he teaches! There's no fluff; just real insight for real people. Inside this book, you'll find advice that is encouraging, approachable, and inspiring."

—Jon Acuff, *New York Times* Bestselling Author, *Do Over* and *All It Takes Is a Goal*

"*Rebel* inspires you to embrace your truest self, talents, creativity, and joy in a world that may resist your authenticity."

—Dan Martell, *Wall Street Journal* Bestselling Author, *Buy Back Your Time*

"Just brilliant! We need more REBELs in the world, and this book gives you the exact framework to uncover your uniqueness and live life your way. You were not meant to fit in a box, and Graham shows you exactly how to emerge from it."

—Dr. Neeta Bhushan, Author, *That Sucked. Now What?*

"Graham does a fantastic job of providing an actionable framework for the reader to live life by design. After reading *Rebel*, I'm giving myself more permission to live my most courageous and joyful life!"

—David Nurse, *Wall Street Journal* Bestselling Author, *Do It*

"This book will mess with you in a good way! If you're ready to uncover and embrace your uniqueness and start living with purpose, passion, and peace in all areas of your life, read *Rebel* and follow Graham's 5-step process."

—Pete Vargas III, Founder, Advance Your Reach

"Our world today is drowning in information but starving for wisdom. I love Graham because he doesn't just help people succeed and create the life they've always wanted; he helps people reach that success without losing their soul. If you're ready for your next level, *Rebel* will show you the way."

—Sean Cannell, Founder, Think Media, and
#1 Bestselling Author, *YouTube Secrets*

"Graham has built a lifestyle that I admire, and it's because he's been intentional in doing things his own way. He's a rebel, and you can be one too (and create a life true to your authentic self) by following his simple 5-step framework!"

—Tom Patterson, Cofounder, Tommy John

"*Rebel* is a road map for anyone seeking to navigate life with intention and create a legacy of influence and impact that inspires others to follow. As a successful entrepreneur and a man committed to generosity and family, Graham isn't just writing this but living it, and it's what drew me to his story in the first place."

—Levi Lusko, Author, *The Last Supper on the Moon*

"This book challenged me to dream again and gave me practical steps to make those dreams a reality. Every time I am around Graham, I am encouraged to think bigger than before. You get that experience from reading *Rebel*."

—Aaron Burke, Author, *The Unfair Advantage*,
and Lead Pastor, Radiant Church, Tampa

REBEL

Also by Graham Cochrane

How to Get Paid for What You Know

Find Yourself by Not Following the Crowd

GRAHAM COCHRANE

Matt Holt Books
An Imprint of BenBella Books, Inc.
Dallas, TX

This book is designed to provide accurate and authoritative information about personal development. Neither the author nor the publisher is engaged in rendering legal, accounting, or other professional services by publishing this book. If any such assistance is required, the services of qualified professionals should be sought. The author and publisher will not be responsible for any liability, loss, or risk incurred as a result of the use and application of any information contained in this book.

Matt Holt is an imprint of BenBella Books, Inc.
10440 N. Central Expressway
Suite 800
Dallas, TX 75231
benbellabooks.com
Send feedback to feedback@benbellabooks.com.

BenBella and *Matt Holt* are federally registered trademarks.

Printed in the United States of America
10 9 8 7 6 5 4 3 2 1

Library of Congress Control Number: 2024004308
ISBN 9781637745656 (hardcover)
ISBN 9781637745663 (electronic)

Editing by Katie Dickman
Copyediting by Michael Fedison
Proofreading by Denise Pangia and Cape Cod Compositors, Inc.
Text design and composition by PerfecType, Nashville, TN
Cover design by Brigid Pearson
Printed by Lake Book Manufacturing

To my bride, Shay. I was a rebel when you married me almost twenty years ago and you've been up for the adventure ever since. Thank you for helping me find myself and for staying by my side all these years. I love you.

CONTENTS

FOREWORD

Deep down inside we know that we are unique, special, and designed for a purpose. But we will never figure out who we are and why we are here if we blindly follow the crowd. The crowd can't give us our identity or show us what we want out of life. That's up to us to discover. And that's why I'm thrilled Graham wrote this book.

When I first met Graham, I knew he was destined to bring a powerful message to the world. We were at an event together and we met over breakfast. I learned two things about Graham that day. First, he and I were both signed to our first book deal by the same person, Matt Holt, whom I've known for twenty years. Second, Graham shared my passion for helping people by writing books and speaking on stages. But it was a few weeks later when he texted me to ask if I'd be willing to coach him for a day that I knew just how serious he was about his mission.

When we finally got together in Tampa at his office to talk all things writing and speaking, I asked him a simple question: "What is the next message you want to share with the world and write about in your next book?" He didn't have a clear answer.

So I pressed him for over two hours, asking him about his dreams, desires, and what he felt most qualified to teach people. While he had a lot of things he could write about next, nothing seemed to click. That is until I asked him to tell me his life story.

As he walked me through his childhood dream of becoming a famous musician and rejecting the idea that he had to go to college and get a "normal" job like his parents and teachers were encouraging him to do, I began to notice a pattern. At each major turning point in his life, Graham refused to follow the crowd, to do what everyone wanted him to do. At some point I interrupted his story, looked him in the eyes, and said: "Graham, you're a rebel! Come on! You even look like James Dean!"

The moment I said the word "rebel," his eyes lit up and I could sense the energy in the room shift.

"You're right!" he said. "That's exactly how I've felt my whole life!"

We quickly began to unpack the patterns of what living as a rebel looked like in Graham's life (and the life of other famous rebels like the ones he lists in chapter two) as he furiously began writing notes in his journal. We discussed how rebels:

- Don't want to be stuck in life
- Choose to create their own future
- Give the world their truest self, filled with all their talents, creativity, and joy

In short, to be a rebel is to create a life on your own terms. And, in reality, it takes courage to create the life, career, and family you want. But it's worth it, and this book will show you how.

From the way he runs his business, to the way he leads his family, to the way he handles his finances, Graham has discovered that he's a rebel himself, and his purpose is to help others become rebels too.

The five-part REBEL framework Graham teaches in this book is simple, practical, and can be applied to any area of life. If you've ever felt stuck, frustrated, or disappointed by how life has turned out so far, this book will give you the clarity, confidence, and inspiration to live your one precious life authentically and uniquely to the fullest.

I'm excited that you've decided to read this book. *Rebel* can change your life for the better, helping you become who you were meant to be. And when you begin to show up fully as yourself and live the Rebel Lifestyle as Graham calls it, you will be able to show up more powerfully in this world. Enjoy the journey!

—Jon Gordon
Fifteen-time bestselling author of
The Energy Bus and *The One Truth*

INTRODUCTION

Why You Need This Book

Most people are living a life that's not even close to being the life of their dreams.

Do you know what the alternative to living the life of your dreams is? Living someone else's dream for your life. Whether a specific person or a nameless, faceless current of culture, someone is shaping the life you are living. Why shouldn't it be you?

At the age of twenty-six, I lost my job during the Great Recession and was on food stamps for eighteen months as I tried to start a business in my spare bedroom so I could pay my mortgage and support my wife and new baby daughter. It was during this dark season of life that I wrestled with two questions: *Who am I, really?* and *What is my purpose in this world?*

Since then, I've been blessed to build multiple seven-figure businesses that require only five hours of work per week, serve an audience of over seven hundred thousand YouTube subscribers, and help ordinary people create incredible incomes online. I even teach how to do all of this in my first book, *How to Get Paid for What You Know.*

SOMETHING WAS MISSING

As I became more successful and both my wealth and impact in the world grew, I realized something was missing—for both myself and my students. We were making money, but were we living the lives we truly felt called to live?

Have you felt that tension yourself? Perhaps you are living parts of your dream, but you feel something is missing. Do you feel stuck in this season of life? Or do you go through your day with a sense that you were made for something more? Something greater?

This is why I wrote *Rebel.* I've discovered that the secret to a fulfilling life is to figure out who you are, what dreams light you up, what you care deeply about, and then unashamedly live as your truest, most authentic self in spite of what everyone around you is doing or saying. In both life and business, I believe that the key to success, satisfaction, and service to others can be summed up in just four words: Do it your way.

THE REBEL'S JOURNEY

To make this a reality, I want to bring you on what I call the Rebel's Journey. I've discovered that there are five key steps that you need to take in order to find yourself fully and step into your purpose. They are as follows:

- **Resolve** to dream again.
- **Establish** the outcomes you want in your life.
- **Break** negative thoughts, habits, and patterns.
- **Engage** in rebellious new thoughts.
- **Let go** of outcomes and others' opinions.

In the pages ahead I will walk you through all five of these steps in detail as you begin to uncover your true identity and live the life you've always wanted. Think of this book as a

The Rebel's Journey

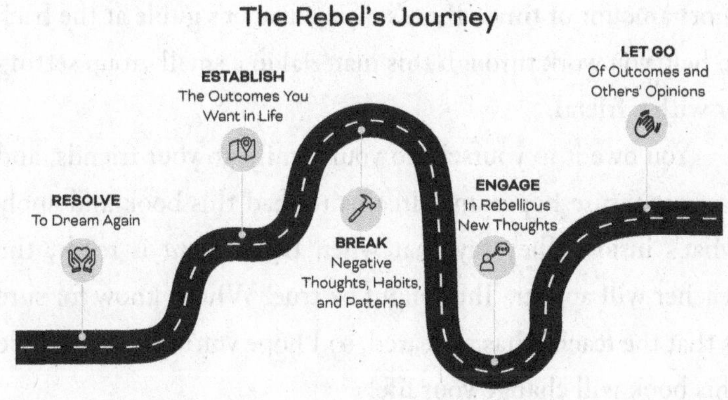
RESOLVE
To Dream Again
ESTABLISH
The Outcomes You
Want in Life
BREAK
Negative
Thoughts, Habits,
and Patterns
ENGAGE
In Rebellious
New Thoughts
LET GO
Of Outcomes and
Others' Opinions

private coaching session with me. In each chapter you will gain new insights about yourself, and after working through the exercises I've provided you will know exactly what next steps to take in your own Rebel Journey.

THIS BOOK IS A QUICK READ

I know you are busy and you likely don't have a ton of time to devote to reading a personal development book like this. So I've written this book with your real life in mind. And by that, I mean it's shorter than most nonfiction books (including my first book).

I did this for a reason: I want you to finish it! More than that, I want you to *do* the book and take massive action on what you learn. Each exercise and discussion question is created for you (not for me) so that you can see massive life change in a short amount of time. There's even a reader's guide at the back to help you work through this material in a small group setting or with a friend.

You owe it to yourself, to your family, to your friends, and to your future hopes and dreams to read this book and apply what's inside. They say that when the student is ready, the teacher will appear. That might be true. What I know for sure is that the teacher has appeared, so I hope you're ready, because this book will change your life!

And finally, as you gain insights and begin your own Rebel Journey, let me know how it's going, take a picture of you with this book, and tag me on Instagram @thegrahamcochrane so I can share it with my community! See you on the other side!

—Graham Cochrane
Tampa, Florida

1

The One Mental Shift That Changes Everything

You are only one insight away from completely changing your life.

It doesn't matter what's in front of you or what's behind you. It doesn't matter what opportunities you have or don't have. It doesn't matter if you even have the energy to change your life right now. Just one mindset shift, one realization of a simple truth can completely change the course of your life.

This might sound crazy or overly confident, but I know this book will change your life. How can I say that? Because this book is about one thing and one thing only: helping you find your authentic self again. Once you know who you truly are, everything else will fall into place.

And as I'll make the case repeatedly in our few moments together, the key to finding yourself is to stop following the crowd—to be a rebel—in every area of life!

And we will begin in this chapter by unpacking one powerful mental shift that (although being incredibly simple) is so profound that you will feel a huge weight lifted off your shoulders immediately, and I believe your level of excitement and expectation for what lies ahead in your life will rise to heights you've never experienced before!

Are you ready? Good! Then let's start with a really important question.

HOW DID I GET HERE?

Have you ever asked yourself that question? I remember the first time I asked it. I was twenty-two years old, sitting in a sad beige cubicle at a small-town rock radio station wearing an oversized dress shirt, goofy tie, and unpolished loafers, wondering how I was going to get any good at selling radio advertising and support my new wife. Not only was I a horrible salesman, but I felt like I was suffocating sitting at a desk all day.

Even more painful, six short months before that, my lifelong dream of signing a record deal and becoming a rock star had died. I'll tell you more about that story (and that dream) in a moment but what I will tell you now is that it was never my goal, plan, or dream to sell ad spots for 98 Rock in Harrisonburg, Virginia. And yet there I was.

It's happened to all of us. Whether in our work, relationships, or finances, we end up in a place we never intended, oftentimes farther away from our picture of what life should be like than we care to admit.

Please ask yourself the following question: "Is this the life I thought I'd be living five years ago? Ten years ago? When I was a kid?"

What comes up for you? Don't judge yourself or be critical of your choices or circumstances. Just acknowledge the reality that you might not be living the life you once imagined you would.

When I talk to friends, family, clients, or even just people online about these deep and important questions, the overwhelming majority of them respond in one of these three ways:

- There is a general disappointment in life (or they just feel bored).
- They feel stuck in a life (or career) they never intended to live.
- There is a vague sense of being made for more but they're not sure what that "more" is exactly.

Do any (or all) of those statements resonate with you?

I personally have felt all three. At many stages of my life I have felt disappointed, stuck, and longed for more. I wrestled with these feelings in college. I wrestled with these feelings in my early twenties when I was broke and on food stamps with a wife, a baby, and a mortgage. What's crazy is that I even wrestled with these feelings when I became a millionaire and had a successful business in my thirties. In every season of my life I have experienced some form of disappointment or discouragement that my life wasn't where I hoped it would be.

WHERE ARE YOU IN YOUR LIFE?

Maybe you are in your thirties or forties and you're starting to question the path you've been on and what you truly value in life. You might be asking questions like: "Is this the type of work/career I really want to do for the rest of my life?" "Do I have to wait another thirty years before I can enjoy life and do what I want?" or, "When did I get so serious and stop having fun?"

Or maybe you're a recent high school or college graduate and you want something different than your parents or peers. You've seen how the paths presented to you have turned out for them and it isn't pretty. You look around at the world online and on social media and know that most of it isn't real and it certainly isn't the life *you* want to live. Or you feel pressure to go in a certain direction in your life and work, but you feel like there are no good alternatives or you will be judged or not supported if you go in your own direction.

Or perhaps you're an empty nester and you want to maximize this next chapter in your life. You have so much more to offer the world and you're ready to stop playing small and finally go for it.

No matter what season of life you find yourself in as you read this book, I think what most of us desperately want is to live our truest, most authentic self, to reach our full potential and feel fully alive.

YOU WERE DESIGNED FOR A PURPOSE

I need to tell you something important. You are not an accident. You were designed by a God who loves you and created you uniquely on purpose, for a purpose. You have gifts, talents, a personality, points of view, and interests that are unique and desperately needed by this world.

I hope I'm not the first person to tell you that, because understanding this truth will help everything else about your life make more sense. You are a piece of a giant global puzzle, and without that piece, the puzzle isn't complete.

The frustrations with life come when we are trying to live out of alignment with our design.

Take my coffee maker for example. I have a nice espresso machine that automatically grinds coffee beans and brews a fresh espresso, coffee, or latte (yes, it even steams milk!). Imagine if my espresso machine saw the blender I have sitting next to it and tried to make a smoothie like my blender can. They both have blades. They both have a top where you can insert food items. And yet, my espresso machine could never make a smoothie, nor should it. It was designed to make espresso, and it's really good at doing just that.

It seems silly if you think about it, but most people operate like that in their lives. They were designed uniquely for a purpose and yet they compare themselves to other people's purposes (or what other people say their purpose *should* be—more on this in the next chapter) and then they feel stuck, frustrated, and out of alignment. Because they are exactly that, out of alignment with who they were created to be.

This happens all the time because we live in a world that publicly celebrates diversity and uniqueness but doesn't actually encourage it—at least not when it comes to passions, skills, personalities, points of view, and interests. Our systems (schools, workplaces, media outlets, and halls of government) tend to produce a vanilla type of person who looks, acts, and thinks one particular way. It's so easy for you and me to turn down the volume of our interests (or mute them altogether) so we blend in and look like everyone else. But that's not very satisfying, is it?

If I may be blunt: Whether a specific person or a nameless, faceless current of culture, *someone* is shaping the life you are living. Why shouldn't it be you?

THE TWO-WAY MIRROR OF MEANING

Not only do we compare ourselves to others, but this is also reinforced by the fact that other people think we should be just like them. There is a fascinating (and frustrating) phenomenon that I call the Two-Way Mirror of Meaning that might help illustrate this for you.

Imagine a two-way mirror like the ones they have in a police station. In one room you have the suspect and one or two police officers asking questions and interrogating him. And on one wall is a giant mirror. At least that's what it looks like to the people in that room. In reality it is a two-way mirror, on the other side of which is a second room where other officers or investigators (or even victims) can look through the glass into the interrogation room.

So, on one side of the two-way mirror you see a reflection, while on the other side you see through the mirror much like a window. Same glass, but you see different things depending on where you stand.

I like to imagine that when it comes to finding purpose and meaning, we are all looking at life through a two-way mirror. We are on the clear side and the rest of the world is on the reflective side. When we look at the mirror for meaning, we see through it to whomever is on the other side. We only see other people, so we naturally compare ourselves to them and try to derive our meaning and identity from what they say, how they act, and what they believe. The result? We begin to look like them.

And this is only reinforced because the rest of the world is on the reflective side of the two-way mirror. When you ask for advice from friends and family about who you are and what your purpose is, they look at you but only see themselves in the mirror. So, without even realizing it, they begin to give you counsel and feedback based on what life looks like for *them* and who *they* are. They unintentionally are too blinded by their own reflections to truly see you for who you are. The Two-Way Mirror of Meaning looks like the diagram below.

Two-Way Mirror of Meaning
WHEN YOU LOOK FOR MEANING, YOU SEE EVERYONE ELSE.
WHEN THEY LOOK AT YOU TO GIVE YOU MEANING, THEY SEE THEMSELVES.

I'm not saying that you can't have people in your life who are able to speak wisdom into your situation. Rather, I'm pointing out the irony of the self-discovery process. When we look to others for meaning, we miss ourselves. And, unfortunately, it's difficult for others to see past their own identities when trying to help you find yours.

The solution is to flip the two-way mirror so you can look closer at yourself. The more accurately you see yourself, the better you'll know who you are and who you were designed to be. And that's when things begin to make sense in life!

IT'S TIME FOR THE REAL YOU TO COME OUT AND PLAY

Søren Kierkegaard, the nineteenth-century Danish philosopher, said: "The most common form of despair is not being who you are."

I believe, deep down inside, you *know* who you truly are and truly want to be. You don't need to become that person. Who you truly are is already inside you and has been since the day you were born. It's just that that version of you has been suppressed. Like I once told a mindset coach of mine: "I think the *real* Graham hasn't come out to play yet."

And get this:

I also believe that you will be the most full of joy, satisfaction, and peace if you operate out of a place of truth and authenticity (who you were designed to be) and not from a place of being who you think you're supposed to be.

This is the one mental shift that changes everything. When you realize that you weren't meant to be anyone or anything other than who God made you to be, everything else starts to make sense!

Author and artist Erwin McManus says in his book *Mindshift:* "It takes great courage for any of us to become the person we're created to be. A huge part of self-leadership is breaking away from the gravitational pull of the opinions of others and finding the courage to become the most unique version of you."

That's what this book is all about—finding your true self, the one that's been covered up for far too long, and operating out of a place of authenticity and alignment with who you were designed and created to be in the first place. And here's the amazing part—when you do that, life gets really fun again!

THE REBEL MANIFESTO

I believe the key to finding yourself is to not follow the crowd, to have the courage, permission, and affirmation to live differently than those around you. In other words, to be a rebel!

- Be a rebel in the way you manage your time and your money.
- Be a rebel in how you parent your kids and love your spouse.
- Be a rebel in the way you take care of your health (physical, mental, and spiritual).

Remember, you will only feel truly alive and aligned when you begin to pivot from what the crowd is doing and live authentically to who you are, in both the big and small areas of life. So, by the end of this book, here is my promise to you. You will:

- Wake up from the world's sleepy autopilot way of living
- Get clear on what makes you unique (and what lights you up)
- Unlearn harmful mental scripts and limiting beliefs that have kept you stuck (potentially for years)
- Have a clear vision of what your ideal life looks like (in your work, business, relationships, finances, health) and how to get there
- Create a clear set of values that can help you navigate the big decisions in life
- Know who you truly are and what you were put on this earth to do

No exaggeration: this book will transform the way you look at your life and make decisions.

And lest you think that this material only works for business owners or single people with few responsibilities, the reality is that this process works no matter what season of life you are in.

- It can help you if you're a stay-at-home parent and feel like your needs and wants are last on the list.
- It can help you if you work a normal 9–5 job and don't feel called to start your own business but still want to contribute to your organization in a deeper way.
- And it can help you if you're still in school and feel like your path is pretty much set in stone.

This book works no matter where you are because where you are is no accident either. You might have lost your spark, your joy, or sense of purpose, but the real you isn't lost. It's just buried under all the layers of cultural drift and life circumstances.

In the next chapter I'll clarify who (and what) we're rebelling against and I'll teach you the five-part REBEL framework to get you unstuck, find yourself, and transform your life. Let's begin!

TAKE THE 30-DAY REBEL CHALLENGE!

I know that life is busy, and many times we pick up a book like this with the best intentions of finishing it and taking action on it. But I know statistically most people won't even read past chapter two.

So to help *you* get fired up and take massive action, and as one more way to say thank you for reading this book, I'd like to offer you something I've developed to help you find yourself and live the Rebel Lifestyle. It's called:

THE 30-DAY REBEL CHALLENGE

Each day for the next thirty days I will email you with an exercise, a quote, a resource, or some good old-fashioned motivation to keep you going on this journey of finding your purpose and making a difference in the world!

Just go to www.grahamcochrane.com/rebelbonus to get instant access to the free 30-Day Rebel Challenge now!

2

The Invisible Force Holding You Back

I was seventeen years old when I realized that I wanted something different than the rest of the world.

It was my senior year of high school and I was pulled into the office of my school guidance counselor. Now, I never had a reason to pop into her office before. Usually she was there to help you manage your stress, think about what classes to take next year, and in general be a support system for you. Fortunately for me, I was sailing through high school pretty easily and was having fun. But this meeting was mandatory.

It turns out part of her job was to help support all of the juniors and seniors in their college application journey and answer any questions they had. As I stepped into her office and sat down on the couch, I immediately felt awkward, like I was in trouble for something. I didn't know what for, but I felt it in the air—the feeling of concern or disappointment.

"Graham, welcome!" my guidance counselor said. "I just wanted to take a few moments today to check in with you and see how the college application process is going!"

You see, for context, all of my classmates had been furiously applying for schools since summer and I hadn't applied for a single one. In our school library there was this giant corkboard where they would post your name and each school you'd been accepted to, and that board was filling up as the weeks went by. It was like a huge "love me" wall for the overachievers and ambitious classmates of mine, with some applying to (and getting accepted by) ten schools or more!

"Oh, gotcha. Well, I'm not planning on going to college," I said. "I want to pursue a career in music after high school. More specifically, I'm going to be a rock star!" Her face said it all. Complete shock and maybe a tad bit of disgust. I could sense the level of concern in the room escalate to code red.

I don't remember her immediate response but she went on and on about how important college is, how it gives you more opportunities down the road, how it would be a great "plan B" if my music career didn't work out, and so on. I listened to her pitch patiently and then calmly reiterated how college would be unnecessary for me as my plan was to do one thing, and one thing only—become a famous musician.

Even though much of that conversation was a blur to me, I will never forget what she said at the end.

"Graham, our school is a college preparatory school and we have a 100 percent college acceptance rate. I honestly don't care what you do after high school but you *must* apply to and be accepted by at least one college."

Wow. There it was. The truth came out. My guidance counselor (and my entire high school for that matter) didn't actually care about me, my dreams, or my unique gifts. Instead, they cared about keeping me on the predetermined path of success for all middle-class American teenagers, which included going to college and getting a "good" job with benefits.

But that's not what *I* wanted.

This actually wasn't the first time I was made aware of the very *Star Wars* Mandalorian cultlike devotion to a prescribed path ("This is the way!"). Growing up in a home with parents who had very traditional jobs (my mom was a schoolteacher and my dad was an engineer), I was told both implicitly and explicitly that the goal was to get good grades in school, go to college, get a degree, and then get a "good" job with benefits.

Side note: when I heard the word "benefits" thrown around when I was younger, I imagined offices with Ping-Pong tables, free donuts, and video game stations in the break room. When I discovered that "benefits" meant insurance and a 401(k), I was even *more* confused as to why I, as a seventeen-year-old, should care!

But in conversations with my dad about *his* career path, it was clear that even he questioned the route he took. He grew up a musician and theater kid, a naturally talented performer. But he gave up on those dreams and instead joined the military and eventually did engineering work for the government. He never seemed to love his job and from time to time would wonder what life would have been like had he pursued his passion instead of following "the way." The pull to follow the prescribed path, the middle-class American way, was too strong for him.

Don't mishear me. I am grateful for my parents. They gave me and my brother a great life. But it was instructive watching my dad wrestle with the tension between his heart's desires and the pull of responsibility.

And in case you were wondering, I *did* end up going to college and getting a "good" job with "benefits." (More on the rock star dream in the next chapter as it's relevant to the work we are going to do together.) But the college decision wouldn't be the only time I was questioned about my choices.

Fast-forward to age twenty-six. I was married, and our first daughter, Chloe, was just born; I had lost a job during the Great Recession and was trying to start an online business around my love for music and recording. I wrote about this journey in my book *How to Get Paid for What You Know*. Long story short, it all worked out in the end and I've never had a job since. But in those early days when we were broke, living on food stamps, and I was scrambling trying to figure out how to build an income online, the absolute hardest part about it was bumping into family members during the holidays.

They would ask *the* question every time: "Graham, why aren't you looking for a traditional job?" And when I answered them with, "Because I don't *want* a traditional job. I'm starting a business," they just stared at me blankly with a mixture of confusion and pity.

Poor Graham, I imagine them thinking. *He's strayed far from* the way.

CONFORMITY: THE INVISIBLE FORCE HOLDING YOU BACK

In each of these scenarios I was bumping up against something very real and very palpable. An invisible force that wanted to suck me back into a clearly defined current or flow that the rest of the world is swimming in. That invisible force is called conformity and I believe it is the thing that will hold you back from the life you truly want to live.

The reality is that most people are living a life that's not even close to the life of their dreams. Their careers, relationships, health, and finances aren't at all what they hoped they would be. And the reason is simple: they've conformed to the pattern of everyone around them.

There is a gravitational pull that is hard to resist. Partially because it's hard to detect! Like a fish swimming in water—it doesn't know that water is all around it because it's invisible and it's all the fish has ever known. Conformity is all around us; it's all we've ever known.

Clearly some conformity is a good thing. We have laws in our country for a reason, and conforming to those laws generally helps keep our world safe and prosperous. For example, I'm sure you would agree that conforming to the laws of property rights (meaning I can't break into your house and take your stuff if I want to) is a good thing! I'm certainly not advocating that we become rebels who take people's wallets or steal people's cars in the name of nonconformity.

Also, as a Christian, I believe that the world and everything in it was created by God, and conforming to God's design for life, relationships, and marriage is a good thing. There's a reason why He set things up the way He did. Life works best when we do things God's way. For example, it's not against the law in my country to cheat on my wife and have an affair with another woman. But in my faith tradition, that would be breaking God's law, and on a practical, human level it would bring pain, hurt, and devastation to my wife and children and ultimately to me as well.

But then there's the world's way. Every culture has predetermined beliefs about what life should look like and what we should value and pursue.

Conformity happens when we have prewritten beliefs about what should be (e.g., what success looks like). That's why my guidance counselor pushed me for college admission. And because she was so insistent, I, too, started to believe that I should go to college. And again, going to college is not a bad thing. It can be a good thing. But not all socially accepted conventions or standards are the right thing for everyone. And yet if everyone around you accepts them as true, it's hard to resist.

You see, no one sets out to conform; we tend to do it by default. And I believe we conform for two big reasons, the first of which is safety or security. Most of us place a high value on safety and certainty, so to break away from conventional norms is scary. The safest thing we could do is keep our heads down, keep quiet, and stay in the pack.

It doesn't feel good to be exposed. It's much easier to blend in and do what those around you are doing. That's why if everyone around you is getting a job, you might keep quiet about your entrepreneurial ambitions. Or if everyone around you sends their kids to school, you might be a bit shy about your decision to homeschool. Or if everyone around you is ordering dessert with their dinner, you might feel prudish by just sticking with a salad. We just want to be accepted and not be the odd man out.

I'm both convicted and inspired by this line in Erwin McManus's brilliant little book *Mindshift:* "You must choose between acceptance and uniqueness. If you're addicted to affirmation, you will become a reflection of yourself rather than the genuine version of you." Yikes! Can't I have both Erwin?! The truth is we can't. Acceptance feels good in the moment, but embracing your uniqueness, finding your true self, is what will ultimately set you free.

Wanting to be accepted by your peers or family is a real issue, but there's another devious reason we conform: it takes more energy not to.

THE SNEAKY SABOTAGE OF AUTOPILOT LIVING

Keep in mind that conformity isn't very obvious. It's something that goes on undetected oftentimes and it happens in the form of autopilot living. If the flow and current of culture is already pulling in one direction (and that current is strong!) then in some ways the easiest thing we could do is flow right along with it. It's the natural tendency. It's our default pattern unless we say otherwise.

When we go about life without questioning the flow of culture or the narrative everyone around us believes, we end up abdicating many decisions to others without realizing it.

Life is busy, our days are full, and we already have a million decisions to make between the time we wake up and the time our heads hit the pillow at night. If you have children, then multiply that decision-making burden by infinity.

The last thing we want to do is make *more* decisions.

Add to that the fact that our brains are so efficient and want to conserve energy, and we end up taking the path of least resistance and allow others to make some of those decisions for us to lighten the load.

Think about your own life thus far. What have been some of the small (or large) decisions that you've abdicated along the way that got you to where you are now? What assumptions have you made about the way "life is supposed to be"? Were there any people you were trying to please along the way?

Here are a few common assumptions we make about life when we live on autopilot that might be worth questioning:

- My kids (or I) have to go to a four-year college.
- I have to work a 9–5 job.
- Couples just argue and that's the way it is.
- My kids (and their happiness) should be the focus of my family.
- I need a bigger/newer house (or car).
- Investing and financial planning is complicated and no one has time for it.
- Debt is normal and is the only way to get ahead.
- Everyone works at least forty hours a week.
- No one really loves their work, just the lucky few.
- I need to be super active on social media to get ahead in my business.
- Having kids will get in the way of my career/life ambitions.
- Getting married will make me feel complete and happy all the time.
- Getting married will cause me to lose myself and my personality.

Do any of those resonate with you? Can you come up with a list of your own assumptions or "outsourced" decisions that you've made in your life up to this point? Don't feel bad if you have. We *all* do this! It's the default human behavior. It's how we cope with the hustle and bustle of our modern world. But as we discussed earlier, it's important to ask yourself: *How is living this way working for me?*

THE SOLUTION? BECOME A REBEL

I believe that ten years from now your life won't be any better or different than it currently is unless you put a stake in the ground and make a change. You must push back against the cultural current of conformity and become a rebel!

But why a rebel? Doesn't that word seem a bit over the top and aggressive? What comes to mind when you hear the word "rebel"?

Perhaps it's James Dean wearing a red leather jacket, smoking a cigarette, carrying a gun, and running from the law in *Rebel Without a Cause.* Or maybe you think about the Rebel Alliance in *Star Wars*, a hodgepodge army with people like Luke Skywalker and Han Solo going to war against a big, bad evil galactic empire.

Here's how the Oxford dictionary defines a rebel: a person who **rises in opposition** or armed resistance **against an established government** or ruler.

And the Cambridge dictionary defines a rebel as: a person who does not like rules or authority, and shows this by **behaving differently from most people in society.**

At a glance, these definitions seem to affirm that James Dean, Han Solo type of lone ranger lifestyle. But look a little deeper and you'll see the "why" behind what makes a rebel. There is something about the established way of doing things in society that they don't agree with. And that is not inherently a bad thing.

You see, rebels go against the grain, they oppose accepted societal norms, and they live life on their terms. It's risky to rebel. It takes courage to create the life, the business, the family that you want. People will challenge you, call you names, and make you feel like an outcast. But the rewards are worth it.

The way I see it:

Being a rebel isn't about getting away with something or breaking the law. Instead, it's about having the courage to give the world your truest, most authentic self, complete with all your talents, creativity, and joy—even if the world pushes back.

REBELS CHANGE THE WORLD

In fact, I believe the world needs *more* rebels. It's the rebels who challenge the status quo and push for change that make our world and culture better for all. Here are just a handful of rebels who have changed history for the better:

- Martin Luther King Jr.
- Steve Jobs
- Rosa Parks
- Amelia Earhart
- Jesus Christ

Each of these rebels was criticized for shaking things up, going against the grain, and not conforming. But they weren't rebels out of selfishness; rather, they were rebels out of creativity and generosity. They each gave something huge to the world, and some of them at a great cost to themselves.

Martin Luther King Jr. and Rosa Parks both believed that conforming to the societal norms of 1950s and 1960s America (norms that included the racist ideology of segregation) was not OK. Against immense pressure and cultural pull, they both chose to peacefully rise up in opposition to the established order of the culture at the time and live differently, not just for themselves but for millions of other Black Americans.

Steve Jobs, cofounder of Apple, launched the Macintosh computer in 1984 in direct opposition to the socially accepted norms of what a computer should be and who should have access to one. The Mac presented a new way of interacting with computers and was geared to normal people, not the intellectual elite. Even the first ever Macintosh commercial depicted a rebel-type figure breaking into a futuristic Orwellian scene where everyone looked the same and stared blankly at the "Big Brother" on a giant screen. She throws a massive hammer into the screen, literally and figuratively shattering the soul-sucking norms of our day and offering a new way of doing things.

Amelia Earhart changed the perception of what a woman could do vocationally in the 1920s (and even wore pants while doing it—another rebellious move at that time).

And Jesus Christ constantly pushed back against commonly held religious beliefs of His day, and made a new way for all people (not just Jews) to be made right with God and have eternal life.

In each of these examples, the rebel was criticized, mocked, judged, and made to feel like an outcast. And yet each one of them changed the world for the better and is highly praised and regarded today.

Steve Jobs even memorialized this concept in one of the greatest commercials of all time called "Think Different." The commercial plays a slideshow of famous world changers from all walks of life and times in history and Jobs narrates this beautiful poem alongside it. Here's just an excerpt that sums it up beautifully:

> *Here's to the crazy ones, the misfits, the rebels, the troublemakers, the round pegs in the square holes . . . the ones who see things differently—they're not fond of rules . . . You can quote them, disagree with them, glorify or vilify them,*

but the only thing you can't do is ignore them because they change things . . . they push the human race forward, and while some may see them as the crazy ones, we see genius, because the ones who are crazy enough to think that they can change the world are the ones who do.

And that's the funny thing about being a rebel. At first, people don't like rebels when they emerge on the scene. Why? Because their actions and words are an indictment of the cultural current that everyone else is swimming in. But eventually, not only do we as a culture come to admire rebels; we want to *be* them.

The books and movies we love are all about rebels who choose to live differently and push back against the norm, and we longingly project ourselves onto them, imagining we could be just like them. Here are just a few examples (spoiler alert on the last one):

- Harry Potter—Much to his muggle aunt and uncle's chagrin, he goes to Hogwarts to become who he really is, a wizard.
- Luke Skywalker—He leaves his uncle and aunt's farm on the desert planet of Tatooine to explore the galaxy and become a Jedi Knight like his father (which is basically a space wizard!).
- Ted Lasso—Pulls the ultimate rebel move by becoming a British soccer coach even though he only knows

American football, and constantly has a positive attitude even when everyone around him tells him he'll fail.
- Katniss Everdeen—She wins the Hunger Games by refusing to kill Peeta and be the last "man" standing and instead threatens to kill herself, forcing the hand of the game organizers to change the rules at the last minute and allow two winners.

Rebels know what they want and have a clear sense of purpose. And we as humans find this attractive. We want that for ourselves, and deep down inside we know we are meant to live this way.

Hopefully you are starting to see what I mean when I say the word "rebel." But so far we've only talked about influential leaders and world changers in history (and some fictional heroes). And being a rebel is not just for "the crazy ones" out *there* doing big things. How does being a rebel play out in the real world of everyday people like you and me?

THE SIX CORE AREAS OF LIFE (SOME GOOD PLACES TO REBEL)

I've learned that there are six core areas of life where we are most likely to conform. Consequently, there are six corresponding core areas of life where we likely want to rebel. Most of our goals, hopes, and desires will fall into these six areas. Let me paint a quick picture of what being a rebel might look like for you in these areas.

- **Work**—Here in America, we are introduced by our names and what we "do" for a living. We are unfairly defined not by who we are but by what we do. While this is unhealthy and problematic, I do think it's critical to actively cast vision for your work and contribution to the world. Your job, work, business, or career is the one area of life where you are likely to spend most of your time. Consequently, for better or for worse, your experience of life will be largely impacted by your experience with your work.

  I'll take it one step further. I believe you were designed by God with gifts, talents, and abilities that are unique to you and given with a purpose in mind. That purpose wasn't just for you, it was for others. You were made to contribute, to serve, to make the world a better place by multiplying your gifts and putting them to work. The principle in scripture is clear: *don't bury your talents* (Matthew 25)! Your work matters, so make sure you are doing the work you were designed to do.
- **Time**—Related to work, how we spend our time (and how we as a culture *value* our time) is complicated. Often, we don't think about how we want to spend our time and so we let others spend it for us. We work long

hours because that's what others do and we assume the extra money we (potentially) earn will make us happier. More on that in a minute.

When not working, we watch TV or stare at our phones to distract us from the monotonous life we have created. This is not only a poor use of our time (trading living our lives for watching other people live theirs) but it's the biggest way we allow the onslaught of conformity to seep into our souls. These days it's rebellious to do things like rest, take a Sabbath or day off of work and phones, or build a business that only requires twenty hours a week to run. But it's worth it.

Time is just as much a currency as money; the only difference is that it's worth infinitely *more*. We can always get more money, but we can never get more time.

- **Finances**—Speaking of money, how has handling it the world's way been going for you? By definition, to conform with your money and possessions in today's society will leave you stressed, in debt, and chained to a job you hate for the rest of your life. Yuck! There's a reason so few people seem to have a genuine handle on their finances and live in peace and contentment with what they own.

  Money is complicated and so is our relationship with it. Depending on how you were raised, you might overvalue money (the more of it you have, the happier you'll be) or undervalue it as if it's more noble or honorable to have few possessions and little wealth. The sweet spot might be somewhere in the middle. But that's not for me to say. Rebelling from the culture's view on how to handle money might look different for each of us, but most of us must rebel.

- **Relationships**—The way we in modern society do family, friendship, and love isn't working. Half of all marriages in the US end in divorce, twenty-four million children grow up in a single parent home, and 60 percent of Americans report feeling lonely on a regular basis. Many families that are intact physically are rarely connected emotionally. With busy sports and activity schedules coupled with both parents working too much, even "stable" homes are producing young adults who don't know how to do relationships well.

  It's hard to choose differently for your family or marriage. When everyone around you is parenting a certain way or treating their spouse a certain way, it almost makes the mess we are in seem normal and OK. To rebel in the way you do relationships will cause people to judge you and look at you differently, but trust me, it's worth it.
- **Health**—You don't have to be a doctor or nutritionist to know that Americans (and many people in

other developed countries) aren't very healthy. We eat the wrong foods, and in mass quantities. We aren't nearly as active as we need to be. We get too little sleep and drink too little water. To put it bluntly, few of us look good naked and many of us will die long before we should, simply because we don't take care of our bodies.

And that doesn't even include our mental health! We stare at screens all day watching the world go by (or at least a version of the world), and we become all the more isolated, depressed, jealous, and detached from reality. Our kids and teenagers are struggling more than ever, and we adults aren't much better off. Our hearts and minds are in pain. These days, to be a rebel simply means to choose health when no one else does.

- **Spirituality**—I'm admittedly not a philosopher or religious studies major, but I find it curious that after a few hundred years of pushing religion and spiritual discussions out of schools, the workplace, and everyday life in general, our world is struggling more than ever in the previously mentioned five domains of life (health, relationships, money, time, and work). We've in effect taken the soul out of our lives and treated ourselves as machines. How's that working out for everyone?

People are starting to figure out that we are spiritual beings having a human experience and in order to live a complete and satisfying life we must tend to the spiritual side of life, not just the physical. For most of human history this was obvious, but our relatively brief three-hundred-plus-year experiment of "enlightenment" and "reason" hasn't delivered what it promised: happiness. Ironically, rebelling in the area of spirituality might look a lot like going back in time to when people fed their souls just as much as their bodies and minds.

Did anything start to come up for you when reading through those six areas? Are you already getting a bit more insight into what your new rebel life might look like? Did you feel yourself nodding along with some of my conclusions? Or perhaps you disagree entirely and are coming to a different conclusion? Whatever it is, keep it in mind and trust your gut. Your reaction is a good indicator of what you value.

FOUR REASONS WE DON'T REBEL

If you look around, you'll see that most people aren't rebels. We all *love* rebels, and deep in our souls we all wish we could *be* a rebel ourselves, but we don't rebel. Why? I believe there are four common reasons.

1. **Social Media**

   We live in a weird time in history. Never before have we had the ability to peer into the lives of millions of other people (famous or unknown) and see how they live, how they think, and what they value—all instantly. And the more awareness we have of what everyone else is doing, the stronger the current of conformity becomes and the more we all tend to look the same and do the same things. Case in point, I'm pretty sure social media is the only reason everyone on the planet now wants to own a labradoodle.

2. **The Desire to Belong**

   We as humans are social creatures. We were made for community. So, whether it's online or in our in-person social circles, there is a natural desire to fit in and belong. It starts early in school and it only continues into adulthood. To rebel would be to leave the safety of the community and that is in conflict with our innate desire to be liked and accepted by those around us.

3. **We Don't Know Any Other Way**

   Like anything you want to accomplish in life, you must have a vision for it ahead of time. Whether it's a vision to build a house, start a business, or raise great kids, you must have a clear path laid out in order to get where you want to go. The reality is that when it comes to living the life of your dreams, there rarely is a clear path laid out for you. You can want to go somewhere, but if you don't know the way, you'll just stay where you are.

4. **It Takes Effort to Be a Rebel**

   At the end of the day, I think the biggest reason we don't take active steps of rebellion and live the life we truly want is because it takes effort. If life is full and busy already, we are most likely to take the path of least resistance, which by definition is the opposite of rebelling. Like I mentioned earlier, conformity is convenient. Being a rebel isn't. But my hope is that this book will convince you that it's worth the effort!

No matter the reason you haven't become a rebel yet, it's all in the past. Today is a new day, and since you've picked up this book, I know that you want more out of life. You owe it to yourself, your family, and those you love to take the next step to living authentically to who you were designed to be and architecting life to align with your values.

But how exactly do you do that? That's where my REBEL framework comes into play.

THE FIVE-PART REBEL FRAMEWORK FOR FINDING YOURSELF AND LIVING YOUR AUTHENTIC LIFE

Like any other transformation you want to see in life, you don't get there in one giant step. To reach your destination of being a rebel and living authentically to who you are, you must break it down into smaller chunks. This not only makes it a more doable process, but at each step of your Rebel Journey you must confront some important truths and learn some critical skills.

But have no fear, I'm here to coach you each step of the way. The remainder of this book will walk you step-by-step through this five-part framework and help you take massive action on living your dream and unlocking your truest self. Here is a preview of the five steps, which conveniently spell out the acronym "REBEL":

R—**Resolve** to dream again.
E—**Establish** the outcomes you want in your life.
B—**Break** negative thoughts, habits, and patterns.
E—**Engage** in rebellious new thoughts.
L—**Let go** of outcomes and others' opinions.

In chapter three, we will begin our rebellious journey to finding yourself by dusting off those old dreams (or discovering new ones). Getting honest about your hopes and dreams will take you closer to the core of what makes you, you. In this chapter I will ask you to do one of the hardest (and most fulfilling) exercises I've ever done personally, the results of which will help shape the rest of your life.

In chapter four, we will get more specific about those dreams. I will take you through another simple but powerful exercise that will uncover what your ideal life looks like in one or all of the six core areas of life.

In chapter five, I will teach you how to identify the false narratives and mental scripts holding you back from the life you want to create so we can obliterate them from your thinking and reprogram your mind.

In chapter six, we will create your new life by changing the way you think, including how to make it easy on yourself to get results. And in chapter seven, we will take the final step of living out the messy reality of being a rebel and how to let go of the opinions of others (including your own opinion of yourself!).

Finally, in chapter eight, I'll share the surprisingly simple way to find your life's purpose and give you a thirty-day action plan to put everything you've learned into practice.

Are you ready to take your first step into the life of being a rebel? Then I'll see you in the next chapter where we will start with the most important step, dreaming again!

3

Dreaming Is the Most Rebellious Thing You Could Do

Step 1: Resolve to Dream Again

In seventh grade my parents moved me from public school to a private school about an hour away. It was hard being the new kid at age twelve because most of my classmates had gone to school together since kindergarten and knew each other well. Plus it was a relatively small school, so there was no way to blend in. Making new friends is never easy, but fortunately for me, on my first day a boy named Rob came up to me and brought me into his friend circle. Within a week, I had a handful of new friends and I was settling in quickly.

That year I got close with two boys in particular, Rob (my first friend there) and James. We had a lot in common including our love of video games, hacky sack, and Magic: The Gathering (a fantasy card game if you care to know; and as you can imagine, girls were lining up to date me). But our deepest shared passion was music.

All three of us loved loud rock concerts, guitars, amplifiers, and songwriting. We started a band together and would have jam sessions in our bedrooms every time we hung out. While other kids would spend their weekends watching TV or playing sports, my friends and I would spend hours writing songs, recording them on my dad's old cassette tape recorder, and then rehearsing them at our drummer's house.

Some of our musical highlights in middle and high school included playing multiple Battle of the Bands, in coffee shops, and even at a local talent scouting event called Star Search. To me, all of this was not only a fun pastime but a training ground for our future of being professional musicians and potentially famous!

But then something strange happened around our junior year of high school, around the same time I had that conversation with my guidance counselor I told you about. As my classmates began talking about college and what life looked like after high school, I remember having a confusing conversation with Rob and James. I don't remember how it came up, but Rob said something to the effect of: "Yeah, I know that I want to eventually go to law school and become a lawyer."

I was confused. "What? A lawyer? Why do you want to become a lawyer?" I asked.

"It's a good job and it pays well," Rob said.

In disbelief I turned to James. "What about you, James? You're still going to pursue music, right?"

James shook his head. "Nah. I'm thinking I'll get into investment banking."

My brain went numb. *What was happening to my friends?! These guys are musicians. They are creatives. Since when did they want to become a lawyer and an investment banker? Is that truly their dream? Or is it their parents' dream? What about having fun? We are seventeen years old for crying out loud!*

I instantly felt alone and confused.

Who knows, maybe those choices truly *were* their dreams. All I know was that in that moment I felt stupid for still wanting to become a famous musician. Their sudden shift from playful childhood to serious and responsible adulthood messed with me.

Should I want their kind of dream too? Was I silly for imagining myself becoming a famous musician? Was that just a fun teenage dream but now it was time for me to grow up like them?

YOUR DREAMS ARE CLUES TO YOUR TRUE SELF

Can you relate to my experience? Did you have a dream when you were younger that got snuffed out because it was time to "grow up"? Have you felt out of place and a bit silly when you've shared your dream in the past, so much so that you quietly put your dream back in a box and buried it deep beneath the surface of your heart?

Maybe you had a dream of what life could be, but somewhere along the way you've "fallen in line" with what everyone around you prescribed as normal and acceptable for someone in your position or at your age. If so, you need to know there's no shame in that. Sometimes life circumstances demand that we let certain things die, at least for a season. Your past choices, even if they involve conformity, do not define you. You did what you had to do, what felt right and made sense at the time.

Or perhaps you don't believe in dreaming. Perhaps you feel that it's selfish to think about and pursue your heart's deepest desires. Sometimes life is too busy, complicated, or just plain hard to have time, energy, or mental space to even think about what we want for ourselves.

But we *must* pay attention to our dreams. Why? They are the first step to finding ourselves. What you dream about is a clue as to what you value and who you truly and uniquely are. So whether you've let your dream die or you feel dreaming is an unnecessary luxury for people with no problems and loads of free time, I want to challenge you to start dreaming again.

And to that end I have good news and bad news. The good news is, there's an inner rebel in you! Starting today you can put your foot down, make a pivot, choose to be different, and begin your rebel life—a life that's aligned with who you really are and what you really want. But here's the bad news: it's taken years to get into the groove of conformity so it will take time (and work) to get out of it.

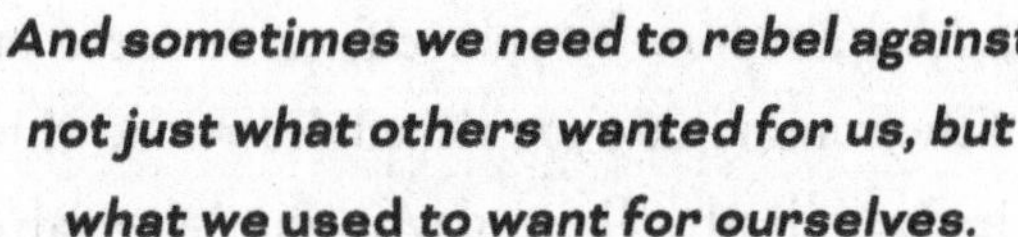

And sometimes we need to rebel against
not just what others wanted for us, but
what we used to want for ourselves.

In his book *48 Days to the Work You Love* author Dan Miller writes, "It's healthy at any point to draw that line in the sand and ask, 'Who am I?' And 'Why am I here?' If you are still living out your life based on decisions made when you were 18, you may have reason to be concerned. Things have changed. You have changed."

But before we can change, and before we can even dream again, we need to acknowledge the fact that it takes courage to stop conforming and be a rebel. It's not easy. You know why? Because it goes against our programming. Not only our biological programming, but also our cultural programming. We've been programmed to fall in line to be safe in society. But this is an outdated program based on an outdated fear.

OUTDATED PROGRAMMING AND MIMETIC DESIRE

Historically, human beings have needed the safety of a community to survive. Falling in line, or conforming to the expectations and rhythms of your village, town, or family farm, was truly a safety mechanism intended to keep you alive. If you stood out, drew attention to yourself, or ventured out of the confines of the community, you risked desertion, which would certainly lead to death. These days, your survival does not depend on you falling in line, and yet we still operate according to that old programming. Even though it doesn't make rational sense, we still want to be accepted as part of the tribe.

There's also a powerful force at play called mimetic desire.

Mimetic desire is desire according to another, or desire according to a model. Imitation is the force that tends to shape human desire. People desire things because someone else—a model—did first. In other words, we want what others want.

We see people drooling over the latest iPhone, so we want it. We see a line of people waiting outside a restaurant and we assume that it must be good and want to eat there ourselves, all because others want to eat there. Even when we shop on Amazon and see those red words near the "buy now" button that say "Only 4 left in stock!" we feel our desire for that item skyrocket. Why? Because other people want it, so much so that it's selling out.

Mimetic desire has always been an issue for humans. But social media has poured lighter fluid on the flame, making us even more likely to conform. This is literally the basis of influencer marketing (a roughly $21 billion market in 2023) and why it's so effective. We want what others want (or say they want). Especially when it's coming from normal people like ourselves and not from the brand directly.

But it's not just other people's stuff that we desire; it's their lives as well. We value what we see others valuing. And with social media we are inundated with people's lives, desires, and opinions, which is only shaping *our* desires and opinions. So much so that we can lose track of who we are and what we really want. This is part of what is leading to so much conformity and discontentment in all of our lives.

Rarely does this conformity lead to happiness. Why? Because we aren't living true to who we are or who we were designed to be.

Dan Miller says it best. "When you get to heaven, God is not going to ask you why you weren't more like Mother Teresa. He's likely to ask you why you weren't more like *you*."

DON'T LET THE MONKEYS PULL YOU DOWN

A lot of times conformity isn't so much about wanting what everyone else wants—it's doing what everyone else is doing even when they don't know *why* they are doing it themselves. It reminds me of the story Dr. John C. Maxwell tells in *The 21 Irrefutable Laws of Leadership*, about an experiment where four monkeys were locked inside a room with a tall pole with bananas on top. One of the monkeys tried to climb the pole to get the bananas and was hit with a blast of water. Each of the other monkeys attempted to climb the pole and were knocked off by the blast as well. Eventually they all quit trying.

The experimenters then replaced one monkey with a new one who, when seeing the banana, immediately tried to climb the pole. Can you guess what happened? The newcomer was pulled down by the others who had been blasted with the water. The experimenters replaced each monkey one by one, and each new one tried to climb the pole but was pulled down by the others. Eventually there were four monkeys that had never been hit with the water. None of them would climb the pole but didn't know why.

So often we let the monkeys in our life pull us down while we're trying to reach for our dreams. And we don't even question it. In fact, none of us question it. We just repeat patterns and behaviors that were modeled for us and so we suck everyone around us into our orbit of conformity or get sucked into theirs.

When you choose to be different, and start to dream again, people will try to pull you down, even though they don't know why.

This was true for me back when I made a decision to work from home and start an online business. Very few people supported me because they had no context for what I was doing. They loved me and they feared for our financial safety as a young family, so they tried to convince me to go get a traditional job. It was hard for them to understand that I didn't *want* a traditional job. I was creating an income for myself in a new and different way.

They weren't doing anything wrong. In fact, they were trying to care for me. But all they knew was the world of being an employee. Me trying to become a digital entrepreneur was like the monkey reaching for the banana that everyone thought was off limits and dangerous. Interestingly enough, after going my own way and starting my online business, many of those people followed suit once they saw it was possible for them as well.

That's one of the wonderful side effects of being a rebel—sometimes you pave the way for another to choose something different and live the life they were created to live as well!

IS IT FOOLISH TO DREAM?

Anyone who has had kids, been around kids, or been a kid themselves (which should cover just about all of us) knows that kids are natural dreamers. We come out of the womb with unlimited creativity and imagination. But I'm talking about more than just the ability to play make-believe. I'm talking about dreams and desires.

At all ages of our childhood and even into early adulthood, each of us has had a dream or two. Dreams of what we wanted to do for a career, dreams of living somewhere amazing, dreams of being loved by someone unconditionally, dreams of having the financial freedom to live the life we truly want.

But somewhere along the way we were told (whether explicitly or implicitly) that it is foolish to dream and we should be realistic. People with genuinely good intentions have an uncanny ability to pull us out of the orbit of dreams and possibility and bring us back "down to earth" where we can be more realistic (i.e., unhappy).

For example, perhaps you feel you've lost the spark in your marriage so you tell your friends that you want to start having a regular weekly date night with your spouse. But then those same "friends" say something to the effect of, "Oh, we tried the date night thing too. It doesn't work. It gets expensive to hire a babysitter each week and eventually you run out of things to talk about. It sounds cute, but it doesn't really help."

In one moment, you got pulled right back down to earth with a healthy dose of discouragement. Simply put, other people can and will squash your dreams, often unintentionally.

But sometimes we squash our *own* dreams. I know I sure did.

I already clued you into this but one of my first big dreams was to be a famous singer/songwriter, make music videos, and tour the world as a musician, and leading up to my senior year of college I was working hard on getting a record deal. Fortunately, I had a songwriting professor who really believed in me. He helped me hire session musicians and a producer from Nashville to help me record an album to shop around to record labels.

I remember being in the studio working with these talented musicians who were helping me record my songs and feeling on top of the world. I was actually making progress on my dream. I felt supported by my professor, and I felt honored and excited to have real musicians playing *my* songs and bringing them to life. My dream was coming true.

I even had a cliché photo shoot for the album cover complete with pictures of me holding my guitar by a brick wall and next to some train tracks, all while looking pensive and deeply creative. I felt legit.

But as we began hearing back from all the record labels we pitched my album to, the best I was offered was a development deal, which meant they would sign me but not pay me until I had developed a bit more and sold albums on my own, proving to them I was a horse worth backing. As I was newly engaged to be married, that wasn't going to work. I needed to make real money to pay my real bills, and so after years of work my dream came to a screeching halt. Want to know the irony of it all? The name of my album was *Pipe Dream*.

Like I mentioned at the beginning of this book, when my rock star dream died and I had to go get a "real job" at the local radio station, I didn't just view it as a bump in the road of my musical journey. I viewed it as the *end* of the road. In order to process my hurt and disappointment, I rewrote the narrative in my mind that dreams are not worth pursuing. I subtly (and likely subconsciously) made a decision to never dream again so as not to get my hopes up. I felt embarrassed and silly for thinking I could make it in music, so I did what most of us do: I went back to conforming like the rest of the world and played it safe.

As much as I'd like to blame others as being dream crushers (and there is certainly plenty of blame to spread around there), much of the time we are our own worst dream crushers.

If our dream doesn't come true, or is taking too long, we can easily begin to minimize what we want and rewrite the narrative so it fits in with the reality we are experiencing.

But here's the sad thing: If we minimize what we want, we will begin to minimize the success we've already experienced, and eventually our ability to dream and pursue a meaningful and satisfying life will diminish. Dreams are like food for our souls, and by starving our dreams we end up starving our souls and our lives.

THE IDENTITY CRISIS INTERSECTION

If you've ever chased a dream that died or never came to fruition, you've likely found yourself at what I call the Identity Crisis Intersection. You might not have known you were at this intersection, but you were there nonetheless.

Think back to a dream you've had that died. It might have been a sudden career change, or a marriage ending, or perhaps like me you pursued a dream of being a famous musician and ran into a wall of "noes." Because dreams are so much a part of our identity, whether we realize it or not, when our dream dies, part of us dies with it. In these moments we can feel confused about who we are as a person.

It's at this moment, right after your dream dies, that you find yourself at the Identity Crisis Intersection. You're at a critical fork in the road and you have two choices in front of you. Two paths you could take, if you will. You can either give up, conclude that dreaming is foolish, and conform. Just be like everyone else and go about your life trying to avoid future pain, embarrassment, and disappointment.

Because dreams are so much a part of our identity, whether we realize it or not, when our dream dies, part of us dies with it.

But there's a second choice available to you. Instead of choosing the path of conformity, you can decide to do something so simple, so obvious, and yet so powerful that people rarely think to do it: you can dream again! The Identity Crisis Intersection looks like the diagram on the next page.

Sure, your dream might have died, but that doesn't mean you can't have a different dream or a different version of that dream. Not all of my dreams have come true or turned out how I hoped. Again, my rock star dream died almost twenty years ago, but I've been living an entirely new dream now that I never thought was possible or even considered pursuing!

The reality is that when I first found myself at my Identity Crisis Intersection I didn't choose to dream again initially. Instead, I conformed. I decided to put my head down and try

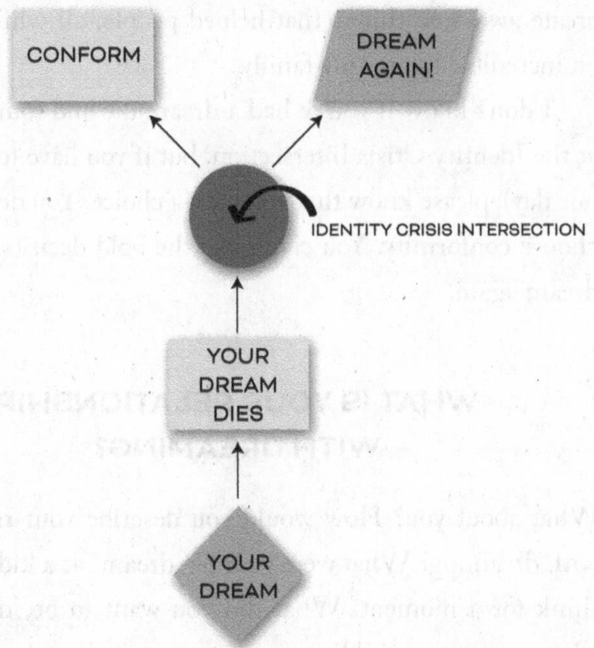

to be like everyone else. I focused on things like being a good husband, father, and employee. I went to church and served in my community. I honestly floated for about four years and it wasn't satisfying. Burying my dreams and denying my desires didn't help me in the slightest.

So, when I found myself at another crossroads at age twenty-six with no job and three mouths to feed, I decided to take the other path that the Identity Crisis Intersection offers.

I chose to dream again. This time, I dreamed of building a business and an income that was flexible and allowed me to create awesome things that helped people, all while building an incredible life for my family.

I don't know if you've had a dream die and found yourself at the Identity Crisis Intersection, but if you have (or if you do one day), please know that you have a choice. You don't need to choose conformity. You can make the bold decision to simply dream again.

WHAT IS YOUR RELATIONSHIP WITH DREAMING?

What about you? How would you describe your relationship with dreaming? What were your big dreams as a kid? Stop and think for a moment. What did you want to be, do, or have when you were a child?

What did you dream about when you were in high school or college? What about when you were first married or had kids of your own? Just take thirty seconds to think back and name one or two dreams that you had.

Now this might be an easier (albeit more painful) question: Where in your life has a dream come crashing down, and have you subtly or subconsciously made an agreement that it's foolish to dream? Another way to ask yourself this question is this:

What has been one of my biggest disappointments in life thus far? Was it a failed relationship or career move? Did something not work out financially as you had hoped? What is that moment of pain where you quietly decided not to hope again, and certainly not to dream again?

Can I just tell you for a moment that I understand? I may not have gone through what you've gone through, but I know what it's like to feel the loss of a dream. And I know what happens to most of us when our dreams are squashed; we become afraid to dream again because we might get hurt or be embarrassed.

It turns out this is our physiological default.

In an article posted on *Medium* entitled "Your Brain Doesn't Want You to Be Happy. It Wants You to Be Safe," Sinem Günel writes that, according to research, "Your brain isn't wired to make you happy. The main purpose of your brain is to keep you safe and make sure you survive. Your body, and particularly your brain, don't care whether you're happy."

And that makes a lot of sense. If safety is your brain's highest value, and you've been hurt by dreaming in the past, then of course you aren't going to want to dream again. The potential for happiness (living your dream) is outweighed by the potential for pain. Just like with investing, people tend to have a stronger negative reaction to losing money than they have a positive reaction to making it. Humans are risk averse by default.

But how is safety (i.e., conformity) working out for you? I imagine if you're like most people, not so well. That's why, even though it can be risky, I truly believe that your unique purpose for being on this planet is meant to be fueled by dreams and desires. Just because you or I have had a dream come crashing down in the past doesn't mean we should give up on dreaming altogether. In fact, the opposite is true.

It's precisely *because* we've been hurt and disappointed by dreams in the past that we need to dream again.

I believe dreams are like food for our souls, and the solution to being hungry isn't to avoid food—it's to go back to the table and feast!

And let me just say, if you are a person who hasn't been able to pursue your dreams because of something external and beyond your control (death, illness, divorce, bankruptcy, single parenting and working three jobs), I see you and I'm sorry.

You haven't done anything wrong. You've just been dealt a very difficult hand of cards. But can I encourage you really quickly? It's not too late to dream again. And it's not impossible to make your dreams a reality. And more importantly, you are too precious and valuable to God *not* to dream and figure out some clues as to who you truly are and what you were put on this earth to do. So please don't move on from this chapter. In fact, you might need it the most!

THE FIFTY DREAMS EXERCISE

This book isn't about theory. It's about action. Because action is what will create life change. So starting in this chapter I'm going to walk you through exercises to apply each of the five steps in the REBEL framework, one step at a time.

Step 1 of the REBEL framework is all about the "R," which stands for Resolve. In order to truly be a rebel, you must resolve to dream again.

The goal of this book is to help you find yourself, break free from conformity, and create the life you want. I'm willing to do my part, but you, my friend, must be willing to do yours. If you truly want life change, you're going to have to partner with me and actually *do* the book, not just read the book.

Now you may have goals for your life, but if you've noticed, we aren't actually talking about goals in this chapter. We're talking about dreams, and there's a difference.

Marcel Schwantes points out in an *Inc.* magazine article that, based on research done at the University of Scranton, 92 percent of people fail to achieve their goals. And while there is a lot of data to support that writing down your goals and making them specific helps you achieve them (more on this in the next chapter), I personally have seen that goals alone are not powerful enough to create life change. Goals are born from dreams, because dreams are where the motivation for change comes from.

Here's what I believe. In order to completely change your life, to be a rebel and go the opposite way of the world around you, to live the meaningful and fulfilling life you were designed for, you need to dream.

Every great thing that was built in the history of humanity, whether a cathedral, a business, or a family, was born out of a desire and a dream.

Dreams have power, because they are based around our desires. Only desire-based dreams have the power to keep you on track with your goals, which will lead to life change.

Dream first, goal-set second.

Now for the exercise. To kick off your Rebel Journey, I'm going to ask you to do some hard (but fun) work. This is an exercise I learned from my friend Cliff Ravenscraft, and it was one of the hardest (and most fulfilling) things I've done. All you will need for this exercise is a legal pad of paper, a fresh page in your journal, or a blank Google document. Then follow these steps:

1. **Write down fifty things you want or desire.** Don't overthink this. Just write whatever immediately comes to mind. If you're getting stumped, ask yourself this question that I stole from Tim Ferriss: *If you were the smartest person in the world and it was*

impossible to fail, what would you dream of doing, being, or having?

For example, you might write down that you want to learn to speak Spanish, or go to Hawaii, or own a home in a specific neighborhood, or become a TEDx speaker. You might want to make enough money to hire a personal chef or fly first class. You might just have a desire to learn how to make crepes. Nothing is too big or too small. Whatever it is that pops in your head, just write it down! Don't judge yourself or curate your thoughts. No one but you will see this.

Full disclosure, this might take you a few days to complete if nothing is flowing very quickly. And that is OK. It took me almost a *week* to come up with a list of fifty things I wanted when I first did this exercise years ago. To get your wheels spinning, here are a few categories to consider dreaming around: work/career, relationships/family, money/finances, health/fitness, hobbies/fun, travel/experiences.

Even if you think you *don't* know what your dreams are, you intuitively know what you want. Author and speaker Bob Goff says in his book *Dream Big*: "For years you've already been quietly curating your life without knowing it. You know what works and what doesn't. What lights you up and what bums you out. What lasts and what disappears."

2. **Create a Top 10 Things You Want from that original list of fifty.**
   After creating your list of fifty things you want, pat yourself on the back real quick, but don't get too excited as you're not done yet. Read back through that list of fifty things and ask yourself: *If I could only have ten of these dreams or desires come true, which would they be?* Write those down in a separate list in no particular order.
3. **Finally, for each of your top 10 desires, answer the question "Why?"**
   Next to each desire (or below), write down why you want to do, be, or have that thing. This is not about justifying your desires to me or yourself or the world. This isn't about moralizing your desires either. Lord knows we have enough people judging everyone else's desires because it's not something *they* personally desire. No, this is a powerful final step to better *understand* your desires.

   Articulating that you want something is powerful. Understanding *why* you want that thing is transformative. Even if the why is simple and obvious, it helps you create more self-awareness. And knowing yourself better is the first step to re-creating your life to be more fulfilling and aligned with your internal makeup.

Congratulations! You've now done deeper self-work than 99 percent of the world's population. This list (while not perfect) is an accurate reflection of who you are, how you were designed, and what you value in life. Of course, the list can and likely will change over time, but right now this is a true snapshot of what makes you, you.

So let me ask you: What surprised you about this list? What showed up on the top 50 or top 10 that you've never fully articulated or imagined you'd want?

Many of us have become so good at suppressing our desires that we aren't even aware of certain core wants that have been lingering under the surface for years.

What *didn't* surprise you about the list? What popped up for you that you've always known was a deep desire and dream of yours, whether big or small? How does it feel to see it written down in front of you in black and white? Does it excite you? Make you nervous or scared? All of those emotions are natural.

What's amazing about this process is that you are actually documenting your desires not just for what we're about to do together throughout the rest of this book but for when "future you" looks back in time.

In preparation to write this chapter, I pulled out the old legal pad I used the last time I did this exercise over three years ago, and looking back through my list of fifty things I wanted back then gave me such a rush of excitement, energy, and motivation. You see, fifteen of those dreams on my list had been realized already! And that includes three of my top ten dreams! It's fired me up to keep chasing those other desires and make them a reality.

There is something powerful about writing down your dreams like this. Something shifts in your heart, mind, and soul when you see your desires staring back at you on a piece of paper or a screen. In that moment of getting it out of your head and onto the page, your dream has taken a huge step forward into the physical world.

In his book *Think and Grow Rich,* Napoleon Hill famously wrote: "Truly thoughts are things." We'll dive deeper into how important your thoughts are in a bit, but just know that the first hurdle to taking a dream from merely a thought or a wish is to write it out in physical (or digital) words so you are forced to see it and acknowledge it.

WHY NOT YOU? WHY NOT YOUR DREAM?

Unless you resolve to live differently than the rest of the people in the world (and how you have been living up until this point) and resolve to dream again, you will never live the life you want. Full stop. No one is coming to rescue you. No one is going to offer you the life you hoped for on a silver platter. The current of conformity in the river of this world is too strong to just hope and float your way to where you want to be.

You have to say otherwise. Enough is enough. It's time to put a stake in the ground and simply *decide* to live the life you were perfectly designed to live. No one will do it for you.

And why not you? You are worth it. You are made in the image and likeness of God. Your dreams are worth it. They have been planted there by God. In fact, I'd argue that on the other side of your dreams, of you becoming all that God made you to be and pursuing all that He designed for you to pursue, is someone else who needs you to be living your authentic self. You are the answer to someone else's prayer, and your dreams are part of what will cause you to show up and serve someone in a powerful way.

And maybe here's an even more profound question: Why not now? Those dreams that you've been putting off? Those desires that you've been silencing? When were you planning on unleashing them? Unless there is a legitimate reason why you can't pursue that dream right now, what are you waiting for? There's rarely a perfect time to do anything in life (get married, have a baby, start a company, run your first marathon). Like the famous Nike slogan, maybe it's time to "just do it"—and do it now!

OK, I know that was a lot. In this chapter we laid the groundwork for change. We dreamed big and got a thirty-thousand-foot view of what fuels us, what makes us who we are. In the next chapter we are going to get super clear on the details of those dreams so they can become a reality.

4

The Best Years of Your Life Framework

Step 2: Establish the Outcomes You Want in Your Life

A few years ago, my wife and I made the very big decision of building a custom home. Our girls had transitioned into a new school near the middle of the city and we were living out in the suburbs. The twice-a-day commute was getting old and we knew after a few months we needed to move in closer. After looking for ten months for an existing home to buy, it became clear that the best option for us would be to build. This turned out to be a much bigger decision than we could have ever imagined.

We had a clear and simple dream: build a house close to the girls' school. But, of course, proximity to their school wasn't all we had on our wish list. We wanted the house to be a certain size, to be on the water, to have a pool, to be Mediterranean Modern in design, and so on. We actually had a full-page document with about twenty-five to thirty bullet points of what our dream house would have and look like.

Now imagine if we handed our builders that one-page document and said, "Please build us this house!" The amazing thing is they could actually build us a house based off of that list. And since they are incredible at what they do, the house they'd build would be incredible too. It would be the size we wanted, have the number of rooms we wanted, would have a pool, and so on. But here's the big question—would the house be what we had in our minds specifically?

Nope. It would be an approximation, a guess. It would be *a* dream house, but it wouldn't be *our* dream.

Why? Simply because we weren't specific enough. In this hypothetical we gave them a rough idea of what we wanted and then let them fill in the gaps and figure out the rest. What happened in reality is that we spent *months* planning out every minute detail of the house from the exact floor plan, window design, and paint color (multiple shades of white in case you wanted to know), down to how many inches above the sink each wall-mounted faucet would be placed in the bathrooms.

My wife and I were so sick of making decisions by the time our design process was over, but all that work was worth it. In the end, our builders knew exactly what to build and where to build it, down to the smallest and most specific of details. We ended up with a blueprint and plan set that was twenty-nine pages in length and a design brief with mock-ups and links to specific products that was almost just as long.

It's not shocking to say that what we ended up with is exactly what we pictured in our minds. We got our dream house because we took the time to think through exactly what we wanted our dream house to be.

YOUR DREAMS ARE LIMITED BY YOUR (LACK OF) VISION

This is the exact same way we create our dream life. Before we live differently or break out of conformity, we need to have a clear picture in our heads of what tangible outcomes we want in our lives. Most people have a general sense of what they want life to look like (happiness, financial security, healthy bodies and relationships, fulfilling work, etc.), but they've never gotten crystal clear about what specifically they envision for their lives and so they never arrive at the goal or even know which way to go to make their dreams a reality.

In many ways we can be quite like Alice in Lewis Carroll's classic tale *Alice's Adventures in Wonderland* when she meets the Cheshire Cat:

> Alice asked the Cheshire Cat, who was sitting in a tree, "What road do I take?"
>
> The cat asked, "Where do you want to go?"
>
> "I don't know," Alice answered.
>
> "Then," said the cat, "it really doesn't matter, does it?"

As we've touched on already, many of us have forgotten how to dream or just given up on dreaming. But even if we *do* become motivated to pursue something better or different, much of the time we chase after our dreams like Alice: looking for help and direction without really knowing where we want to go.

Think for a moment about how unhelpful it would be to ask a financial planner for advice on becoming wealthy when you haven't gotten clear on what "wealthy" means to you. She would likely ask you a ton of clarifying questions about how much money it takes to fund your ideal lifestyle, how much money you have in your investments already, what your hopes and dreams are for retirement, and so on.

Or imagine getting in your car for a road trip and asking your GPS or maps app of choice to take you to "the beach." Which beach would it take you to? Would it just pick one for you? And would you be happy when you got there (wherever "there" is)?

I get approached all the time by friends and strangers alike asking for generic "help" in their businesses. My ability to help get someone incredible results in their business is predicated on them having done the work of crafting a clear vision of what they want to *create* in their business in the first place.

The power of tools and advice from people lies in your clarity of vision. There are resources out there ready to help you, but they can only help you but so much if you don't know the destination.

In the Bible, God tells the prophet Habakkuk to "write the vision and make it plain" (see Habakkuk 2:2 ESV). The Hebrew word there for "plain" means "to make it clear." And famously, King Solomon wrote, "Where there is no vision, the people perish" (Proverbs 29:18 KJV). The word for "perish" in Aramaic means "to be empty or vacant." Said another way, without a vision, your life is empty or void.

You can dream all you want, but without a clear vision, all you have is an empty dream. That's not what I want for you.

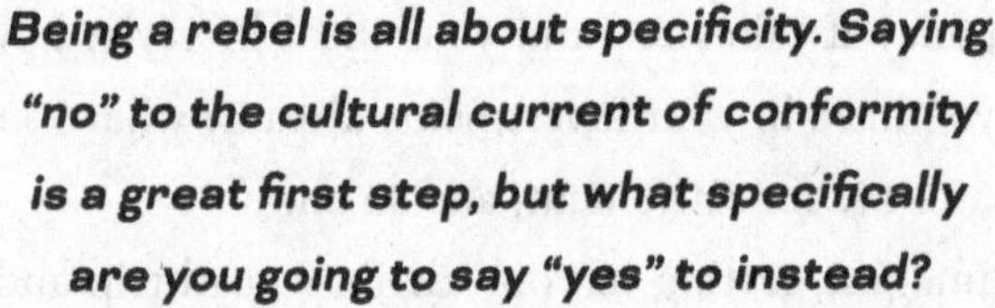

Being a rebel is all about specificity. Saying
"no" to the cultural current of conformity
is a great first step, but what specifically
are you going to say "yes" to instead?

And that's what we are going to do together in this chapter: we are going to create a vision for your life. If you've never done this before, it will be a powerful experience. If you already have a life vision but feel you've gotten off track in pursuit of it, this will help realign things. We will get specific and granular so we have a clear visual (hence the word "vision") of what your new life looks like.

Right now, I'm going to walk you through another exercise that I normally take my private clients through. It will help unlock your dreams with uncanny clarity.

THE BEST THREE YEARS EXERCISE

In the last chapter we covered Step 1 of the REBEL framework: we resolved to dream again. Now it's time to get specific. In Step 2 we cover the first "E" in REBEL, which stands for Establish. In order for your dreams (and new life) to become a reality, you must establish the specific outcomes you want in your life.

Remember how I had to create a blueprint for my custom home before the builders could begin the construction process? The same is true for your life. It's time to create a blueprint for the life you intend to build. And to do that we are going to open up your imagination a bit more with something high-performance coach Rich Litvin calls the "Best 3 Years Exercise." I learned this from him and I find it incredibly helpful for both myself and my private coaching clients.

In this exercise we are going to peer into the future a bit, your ideal future, take a look around, and note all the details of what makes that future amazing. The power of this exercise is the time frame of three years as well as the framing of the question. I suggest you give yourself at least twenty minutes to complete this exercise. Please don't rush it, as the magic comes from giving yourself time to unpack your answer to the question with as much detail and creativity as possible. Are you ready?

Grab your journal, legal pad, or Google doc from the last chapter and then answer the following question:

If we were to meet up three years from now (for example, we bump into each other at a coffee shop, on an airplane, or at a conference) and I asked you how you've been and you told me,* "Graham, this has been the best three years of my life!" *what would you be telling me about?

Just brain dump everything that comes to mind. What would have to be true for the next three years to have been the best three years of your life? If you get stuck, consider reflecting on those six core areas of life we unpacked in chapter two. What (if anything) related to those areas is going amazingly? Why is that? Don't hold anything back and be as specific as possible.

You might start out with some broad-stroke highlights of why these past three (future?) years have been the best of your life. Go deeper. Explain to me the specifics. Ten people doing this exercise might say they've "found the love of their life" as one thing that's been great, but the nuances of that relationship and why it's so great will be vastly different for all ten. The goal is to be honest and deeply personal.

There are a few reasons why this exercise is so powerful:

- **It gets you to project only three years into the future.** It's not so far in the distance that you have absolutely no clue what will be happening in your life. We all will likely be very different people ten years from now. But three years from now you will be very close to who you are now. But three years is also long enough to have some major life change in all six areas of life.
- **It gets you to think in terms of past tense.** Instead of peering into the future and "hoping" or "wishing" your life could be different, you are doing some basic visualizations and then articulating things as if they have already happened. You're basically experiencing them (or retelling them to me) as you would a memory. This makes it more real and concrete and opens up new

neural pathways in your brain that expand your creativity and ability to be open to new things.

- **It's completely open-ended.** Instead of asking a leading question like "How much money do you want to be making?" or "What weight do you want to be?" this exercise allows *you* to define what would make these next three years the best of your life. This is different for everyone. It also allows your subconscious to "speak up" and draw your attention to what truly makes you happy as opposed to what you *think* would make you happy.

  For example, many times my coaching clients want to make a lot more money in their business in the future, and if I ask them money-related questions, they will give me specific answers of how much money they think will make them happy. But when I have them go through this open-ended exercise, many times what comes to mind for them has nothing to do with finances, but rather they imagine how they are spending their time and what family life looks like.

So, if you haven't yet completed the exercise, I beg you to pause on reading any further, and take the next twenty minutes minimum to journal out the answers to the question. Go ahead. Don't worry. I won't go anywhere.

Seriously . . . please do it.

OK, now that you've done the exercise (you *did* do it, right?!), did anything surprise you about your response? Did you have anything seemingly come out of nowhere? How about your fifty dreams from the last chapter? Did any of them come back up in this vision? Did you get any clarity on an area of life that matters to you more than you might have previously told yourself?

LET'S ZOOM IN ON YOUR IDEAL DAY

I truly want the next three years to be the best three years of your life, but in order to make that happen we need to focus a bit more and keep zooming in. You see, it's almost impossible to change your life in all six areas at once. Realistically you can focus on two to three areas at any given moment. What I don't want to happen is that you read this book, have a brief flash of motivation, and begin trying to rebel in every area of your life, only to lose steam thirty days from now and be right back where you are, swimming in the sea of conformity.

The important question for you right now is, *What area in your life do you want to break free from conformity the most right now? In which area do you want to start creating something new?*

Moving forward in this book, we are going to zero in on this one area of your life that you want to change. The one pressing dream you want to bring into reality. Of course you can and will rebel in every area you need to and your entire life will change over time, but for now I want you to put the five-step REBEL framework into practice so you can see how it works by picking one thing to change.

Is it in your relationships? Your health? Your finances or work? Whatever area you choose to focus on for now, perhaps go back to your list of fifty dreams (or just your top 10) and pick one of them that you want to make a reality in the next few weeks and months. What I want you to do next is to go super detailed on that dream and journal out answers to the following questions:

- What does your ideal day look like after this dream has come true?
- What do you spend your time doing?
- Who are you spending your time with?
- How do you feel as you lay your head back down on your pillow after your ideal day?

It might help to find a quiet place (hopefully it's quiet where you're reading this book right now!), close your eyes, take four big, deep breaths in and out, and then begin to visualize your ideal day. Spend five minutes imagining yourself going through your day from when you wake up to when you drift off to sleep, but all from the perspective of your dream outcome in this one area having already happened. Imagine it like a memory.

Here is an example.

Let's say one of my fifty dreams was to get in the best shape of my life, and in my best three years vision I was at my lowest weight and body fat percentage I'd ever been. In this vision I'm strong, lean, and confident with my shirt off when I go to the beach or pool. If I were to zoom in on my ideal day after this dream has come true, I might jot down the following answers to the questions:

- I wake up at 5 AM fully rested and refreshed (because I went to bed at 9 PM the night before as always, now that I'm committed to getting a full eight hours of sleep each night).
- I get in a sixty-minute workout before my family is even awake.
- I eat a healthy breakfast consisting mainly of a protein-packed fruit smoothie.
- I have plenty of energy throughout the day at work.
- I get at least ten thousand steps in each day.
- I take a brisk thirty-minute walk during my lunch break to get more steps in.
- I am home before dinner.
- I cook/order/prepare a healthy dinner with my family without any screens or tech present at the table.
- I spend time connecting with my wife/kids/family.
- I wind down with a good book or time writing in my journal.

- My head hits the pillow at 9 PM and I feel empowered, energized, and excited for the next day.
- I am committed to making healthier food swaps, tracking my calories and macros, and having a couple of cheat meals on Saturdays.
- I've found an active hobby I can incorporate to get into shape faster while having fun outside of the gym.
- I read one health/fitness/food book a month to get new ideas and continue to change my physique.
- I have a workout buddy for accountability and encouragement.

EVERY DREAM IS CREATED TWICE

Do you see what we did there? We took one simple dream (get in the best shape of my life) and broke it down into a daily blueprint that we actually would enjoy. We got specific and envisioned the day as if it were a reality. If you were in the best shape of your life, your day would likely look different than it does now. It would *have* to. This isn't magic. It's life change.

Conformity is taking your physique and health in one direction, so you must rebel and go in a different direction. Not just theoretically, but day by day in the real world you must (and will) make different choices. So your job right now is to paint the picture in vivid detail so you know what to shoot for when building the life of your dreams.

As Robin Sharma famously said in his book *The Monk Who Sold His Ferrari*: "Everything is created twice, first in the mind and then in reality." If you want to create the life of your dreams, it must be first created in your mind. We've begun that process already. But there are some barriers that lie in the way of your dream life being created in reality.

In the next chapter we will identify the limiting beliefs, thoughts, and patterns that are holding your dreams back. Think of this as the demolition work of a home renovation project. Before you can bring your dream house design to life, you must first demolish the old, janky structure that exists today. In short, it's time to get your hands dirty.

5

Reprogram Your Mind with the Inner Story Audit

Step 3: Break Negative Thoughts, Habits, and Patterns

Before I ever started a business, coached high performers, wrote books, or spoke on stages, I was a musician. On top of playing and writing music, I was an audio engineer by trade. I actually went to college to learn how to record and produce music and in the process fell in love with a piece of software called Pro Tools.

Pro Tools (originally created by Digidesign and now owned by Avid) has been the industry-leading computer program in modern recording studios since 1991 and pioneered much of the software-based music production boom we are seeing in the world today. However, around the year 2011, when Pro Tools version 10 was released, this "Industry Leader" was looking more like a dinosaur when it came to its competitors. The software was clunky, slow, and couldn't do half of what some of the newer programs were doing at a fraction of the price.

In many ways, Pro Tools 10 was a disappointment. It wasn't that the designers at Avid weren't aware that they were losing market share to their younger, newer competitors. It wasn't that they didn't know what new features their customers wanted. In fact, the people who make Pro Tools use the software themselves in many cases, so they had the same list of fixes and feature requests that their users did. So why hadn't the software progressed like it should?

Two words: old code.

Most of the features users wanted as well as the overall improvement in speed and processing that was desperately needed were literally impossible to implement on the old code. In a nutshell, what Avid had been doing since the early 1990s was adding code on top of the existing architecture, much like adding a room onto a preexisting house. It worked fine for a while, until it didn't.

For two decades Avid was adding on to the old code to make the software "look" shiny and new, but underneath the slick veneer was a clunky, slow, and outdated piece of software. This "add on" approach reached its limit at version 10 when it launched in 2011. In many ways that release was a stall tactic as behind closed doors they were actually hard at work at rewriting Pro Tools from the ground up. This was a long and expensive process, but the result was worth it.

In 2013, Avid released Pro Tools 11 to the world with great fanfare. For the first time, twenty-two years after the release of Pro Tools version 1, they brought something truly new to the marketplace. And it was finally what we needed. It was fast, powerful, and easy to use. Consequently, in the decade since, Avid has been able to regain some of the market share it had lost and reestablish itself as a dominant platform in home and pro recording studios around the world.

Why should you care about this audio software history lesson? Just like Pro Tools:

You and I are walking around with a bunch of old code; many of us have been running on the same old, crusty, outdated programming for twenty, thirty, even forty years!

Assuming you have at least twenty years of old code and programming as the foundation for your life, can you begin to see how hard it will be to make any lasting change without a major overhaul of your operating system? I'll confidently say it is virtually impossible to build a new, incredible life on your old platform. You must first break the old code before building the new.

It's not enough to know where you are going in life (the outcomes we established in the last chapter). You first have to undo years of bad habits, programming, and negative self-talk.

WE BECOME WHAT WE THINK ABOUT

While you and I aren't machines, we do have programming. And that programming is made up of our thoughts. Everything we do or hope to do in our lives begins in our minds. For better or for worse, our minds are the factories where our lives are created. So that raises the question: What's going on in your mind right now?

Another way to ask this question is: What do you think about? What thoughts are constantly running through your head? Are they positive? Negative? Do you even know what you think about on a daily, hourly, minute-by-minute basis?

There is a lot of science being done right now on the power of our thoughts and our overall mindset (which we won't get into here), but at its most basic level it's important to understand that your thoughts affect your life.

In the old King James translation of the Bible, King Solomon writes in Proverbs 23:7: "For as he thinketh in his heart, so is he." In 1956, motivational speaker Earl Nightingale recorded what would later go on to be his most popular piece, *The Strangest Secret* (selling over one million copies), in which he famously describes what he thought was the most amazing "secret" in the world: "We become what we think about most of the time."

> *The human mind is much like a farmer's land. The land gives the farmer a choice. He may plant in that land whatever he chooses. The land doesn't care what is planted. It's up to the farmer to make the decision. The mind, like the land, will return what you plant, but it doesn't care what you plant.*
>
> *If the farmer plants two seeds—one a seed of corn, the other nightshade, a deadly poison, waters and takes care of the land, what will happen? Remember, the land doesn't care. It will return poison in just as wonderful abundance as it will corn. So up come the two plants—one*

corn, one poison as it's written in the Bible, "As ye sow, so shall ye reap."

The human mind is far more fertile, far more incredible and mysterious than the land, but it works the same way. It doesn't care what we plant . . . success . . . or failure. A concrete, worthwhile goal . . . or confusion, misunderstanding, fear, anxiety, and so on. But what we plant, it must return to us.

—Earl Nightingale, *The Strangest Secret*

What comes up for you as you hear that analogy of planting seeds of thoughts in your mind? Are you planting good thoughts? Or negative thoughts? Are you planting thoughts that lead to the life you truly want? Or thoughts that lead to the life you currently have?

If you're like most people, it's a mixed bag. We typically have a lot of voices and thoughts running through our heads, but generally there are two dominant voices. The key is to know which ones to listen to.

TALK TO YOURSELF, DON'T LISTEN TO YOURSELF

Over the years I've come to discover that on any given day in any given situation there are two main voices in your head: your intuition and your inner story. I like to say that your intuition is like a still, small voice. It's there, it's clear, but it's quiet and oftentimes hard to hear.

If you are a person of faith, this still, small voice is usually God's voice as He often leads and guides you with nothing more than a whisper. There's a scene in the Bible where God is speaking to the prophet Elijah, but it's not in the way even he expected:

> Then [God] said, "Go out, and stand on the mountain before the LORD." And behold, the LORD passed by, and a great and strong wind tore into the mountains and broke the rocks in pieces before the LORD, but the LORD was not in the wind; and after the wind an earthquake, but the LORD was not in the earthquake; and after the earthquake a fire, but the LORD was not in the fire; and after the fire *a still small voice.*
>
> —(1 Kings 19:11–12 NKJV, emphasis mine)

Your inner story, however, is the opposite of the still, small voice. It's loud and stubborn. Consequently, it's hard to hear the still, small voice of clarity and wisdom as it's usually drowned out by the default inner story that is louder. Add to that the fact that you are hardwired to want to listen to and prove that loud inner story to be true.

In his book *The Latte Factor*, author David Bach tells this story of being by his grandmother Rose Bach's bedside as she was nearing the end of her life. At the end of a conversation about if she had any regrets in her life, David's grandmother Rose says,

> "David, don't have regrets later in life. Take the risk. And remember this," she added. "When you get to your fork in the road, you will hear two voices: the big-boy voice that says, 'Be safe, go the safe road!' And the little-boy voice that says, 'David, go This way! It'll be fun! Let's try!' That voice, the little-boy voice, the one that's excited and wants to play—let that little boy come out and play. And tell your friends to do the same."

It's critical to remember that the still, small voice (or the little-boy voice) is easy to miss and often gets overlooked. In her book *The Game of Life and How to Play It* author and spiritual teacher Florence Scovel Shinn says that usually the answer you need in a critical moment "will come through intuition (or hunch); a chance remark from someone, or a passage in a book." My hope is that something in *this* book will be that still, small voice for you, guiding you to a place you deeply long to go.

The key to hearing your intuitive still, small voice is to quiet the much louder inner story.

The first step in this process is to stop listening to yourself. Listening to yourself means you will most likely hear the loud inner story, which is the default narrative you are telling yourself. Rather, you need to start *talking* to yourself. Talking to yourself is telling yourself a *new* narrative, planting *new* thoughts—more on that in the next chapter, but first a look at some of the most common existing narratives.

FIVE COMMON MENTAL SCRIPTS POTENTIALLY HOLDING YOU BACK

For now, it's important to recognize and call out the loud and stubborn default narrative, the old inner story that is holding you back and leading you to conform. And while each of us has a unique narrative running through our heads, there are a few common ones many people suffer from.

Here are five of the most insidious mental scripts we recite, like lines from a movie screenplay. These are the lies we tell ourselves (and we are very convincing) that keep us safe in our bubble of conformity, never making progress toward our dreams. See if one of these rings true for you.

1. **"I'm not smart enough to . . ."**
   Whether it's switching careers or buying your first house, a dream can come to a screeching halt if you believe that you are somehow unqualified in the realm of intelligence to pull it off. Most of the time it's not really that we think we are dumb or unintelligent; rather, it's a vague sense that we don't have enough

information (or the *right* information) to successfully venture off in this new direction.

While super common, this mental script is easy to dismantle. We live in the most knowledge-abundant time in human history where literally anything you would ever need to know in order to take meaningful steps toward your dream is at your fingertips with a simple Google search.

One quick example: I felt like I wasn't clued in enough to become a published author. So I started searching for information on how to get published. That search led to an online course by Michael Hyatt called *Get Published* (great name!), which gave me enough confidence to begin the proposal writing process. Everything else snowballed from there and two years later my first book was released with a major publisher!

2. **"It's too late to try something new . . ."**

   Feel like the clock is running out on your chance for your dream? Welcome to the club. For some reason many of us, no matter our age or season of life, feel like we are late to the party. Whether it's your dream to build your first $1M nest egg or learn to speak Spanish, we assume that time is not on our side.

   Part of this mental script is good old-fashioned laziness. It's an easy out to say there's just not enough time. But the reality is the opposite. You will never have *more* time than you have now! I know it's a bit morose to talk about death, but it's coming for us all. Each day you wait, you are by definition giving yourself less time. So feeling like it's too late for you to work toward your dream is somewhat pointless. You can't go back in time and start five years ago. Today is your next best option. So why not start today? Why not now?

Just for inspiration, here are a few people who found big success late in life. Designer Vera Wang didn't start her career in the fashion industry until she was forty. Julia Child didn't publish her first cookbook until age fifty. And actor George Burns didn't win his first Oscar until he was eighty! If you still have breath in your lungs then it's never too late to start something new or keep chasing that dream!

3. **"If I ________, this is what is going to happen."** Many times we talk ourselves out of life change because we're convinced something bad will happen as a result. There will be some fallout or negative consequence that makes our dream not worth the supposed cost required. We say in our minds, for example: *If I quit my job to pursue a work-from-home business so I can spend more time with my kids, I'll ruin my resumé should my business not work out and I'll need to go get another job.* Maybe. Maybe not.

The problem with this assumption is exactly the fact that it's an assumption. We actually don't know what will happen. Julia Woods, an expert couples coach, taught me there are three realms of knowledge: what we *know* we know, what we know we *don't* know, and what we *don't know* that we *don't know.*

Telling yourself what will happen in the future is actually pretty arrogant. You might have an idea of what *might* happen (everything that could go wrong goes wrong), but you also don't know what you don't know about the situation, meaning there are endless possibilities. Including endless *positive* possibilities and outcomes. Being a rebel means taking the risk to see what's on the other side.

4. **"I don't have enough resources/money/connections/time . . ."**

This script is similar to the "not smart enough" excuse. You might be excited to create a life that is more aligned with your talents, desires, and personality, but as you look around you feel sorely ill-resourced to accomplish your goals. For example, as a business coach I hear all the time how little time or money people have and thus they can't start a life-changing business. They assume their lack of resources will be prohibitive for them. Rarely is that the case.

Much like how we dismantled the previous script, if you feel limited in time, money, or connections you simply need to get curious about what you don't know you don't know. You might *know* that you don't have enough money right now for a down payment on your dream home, but perhaps you don't know what you *don't know* about current first-time home buyer programs or grants or even an unexpected inheritance from your great-aunt Sally who just passed (may she rest in peace!).

The reality is there are *so* many ways to make a dream come true. The trick is to stay open and curious, moving your brain out of the limiting mental rut of the way you currently see things from your vantage point.

5. **"If I do __________, people will judge me."**

Finally, we come to one of the most insidious of all mental scripts: fear of judgment. This might be the most powerful one of them all simply because we all too easily give other people way more power over us than we should. This mental script sounds something like: "If I become a stay-at-home dad, people will think I'm lazy and not a real man." Or, "If I buy that car (or that house, or take that vacation), my friends and family will think I'm greedy and materialistic."

Author and business mentor Mike Zeller says this about judgment: "When you live in fear of judgment by another, you also handcuff yourself from receiving more good, especially if that thing they are judging is what you want (more wealth, love, joy, freedom, etc.). The reality is people will judge you no matter what, so you might as well be fully you in all the wonderful ways God has made you."

I couldn't agree more. This fear is real because there's no way to stop people from judging you. In fact, they likely will. But whose life are you living anyway? Theirs? Or yours? Remember, conformity (what they want from you) isn't working for them. So be a rebel and do the thing anyway!

THE INNER STORY AUDIT

Did one of those five mental scripts resonate with you? Anything sound familiar or hit home? If so, congrats and welcome to the club. I've struggled with all five myself! I say congratulations are in order because having some self-awareness of the loud inner story is a critical first step to becoming the life-loving rebel you were born to be.

And before we wrap up this chapter, I want to give you a simple tool that you can use to get even more crystal clear about the specific narrative that is going on in your head. It's called the Inner Story Audit and it's worth spending the next twenty minutes journaling out your responses to complete the following prompts. You'll want to take the time to do this work because it will make recognizing the loud, stubborn narrative that much easier in the future when it comes up again as you move closer and closer to your dream.

Keep your answers somewhere easily accessible so you can review them often. This in a way becomes a sort of self-counseling and reorienting resource as you come up against mental resistance in the months and years ahead. Here are the prompts:

- **The story I'm telling myself about ________ is:** Go into as much detail as you can here. Be honest, and don't shame or judge yourself for thinking this way. It's just a data point, a way you currently see things. We have to be honest and aware of what obstacles will be in our way.
- **The daily actions/habits I'm taking that reinforce that story are ________:** Now try and pinpoint what tangible ways you are making yourself "right" about that inner story. How in the physical world are you acting out your story? Where do you see it show up on most days?
- **The people around me who are negatively reinforcing that story are ________:** Don't be alarmed. We aren't planning on ending relationships or having someone "taken care of" just

because they are a negative influence on us. However, it's important to be aware of who is subtly reinforcing your negative thoughts and "agreeing" with your mental scripts so you can either limit how much time you spend with them or at least mentally prepare for what they might say or do that could get you off course.

- **The results I'm getting from telling myself this story are ________:**
  You likely already know this, but it's powerful to write out in plain English what the cost of believing and living your default inner story is. What "results" is that story giving you? Do you like those results?
- **What else could be as true, if not *more* true, than the story I'm telling myself?**
  This question forces your mind to get curious, to wonder about what we don't know. You might get stuck here, but don't overthink it. Just write down other potential possibilities or realities that might exist.
- **What are the three to five negative thoughts, habits, or people that I need to eliminate from my day-to-day life?**
  This one is pretty straightforward. When looking back at your answers to the previous questions, what needs to be eliminated from your daily life in order to make room for the new thoughts, habits, and people that you will introduce moving forward?

I'm proud of you. You've done some of the hardest inner work you could do that will lead to incredible life change! In the next chapter we will begin to take steps toward becoming your authentic self, to swim upstream from the current of conformity, and actually live the life you were designed for.

6

The Life Change Formula: Believe, Think, Feel, Do

Step 4: Engage in Rebellious New Thoughts

For years I had a dream of giving a TEDx talk. If you're not familiar, TED is one of the most well-respected stages and brands in the world featuring some of the greatest minds, leaders, and speakers sharing "Ideas Worth Spreading," as their tagline says. TED and TEDx talks are historically eighteen minutes or less in length and are designed to get the audience to think differently and take action in their own lives. I personally love watching TEDx talks and always dreamed of becoming a TEDx speaker myself.

But for years, that's all my TEDx talk ever was—a dream. I didn't know how to make it a reality. So, in 2022, I committed to my vision of landing a TEDx talk. Because I didn't know the first thing about the process, I hired a coaching group that specializes in helping its clients write, land, and deliver a successful TEDx talk. A big part of the coaching process are these daylong intensives.

I remember the very first intensive during which they broke down the process of how to come up with your talk idea and pitch it to TEDx event organizers. They explained how everyone has an idea worth spreading and that each of us had a powerful TEDx talk inside of us. They also shared the fact that it takes their clients on average eighty-six applications to TEDx events to land a "yes." As they described the process, they explained that if you set up your applications the way they teach, landing a TEDx talk was only a matter of math, not luck!

All of this made so much sense to me and I walked away from that daylong session energized and feeling like my dream of becoming a TEDx speaker was not only possible, but inevitable! Infused with that confidence and belief in the process, I committed to landing my talk in 120 days. I wrote it down in my journal. I told my wife, kids, parents, and friends. I even told my customers and social media followers that I was pursuing a TEDx talk.

I applied what the coaching group had taught me about presenting my talk idea to event organizers in a strategic way and I committed to applying to one hundred events, knowing the average was eighty-six applications to land a talk. Each week I sent in five to ten applications. Nothing happened for three months (except for the occasional polite rejection email), but as I entered my fourth month of the process, on my seventieth application submission I received the email I had been waiting for: "You've been selected to speak at our TEDx event!" It worked!

Three short months later, I flew up to Philadelphia to deliver my TEDx talk ("Why Givers Are Happier and Have Less Money Stress"), and now it's on the official TEDx YouTube channel for all the world to see! My dream came true! I am a TEDx speaker!

Now let me ask you a question: Can you spot what was the most important moment in my TEDx dream journey that made it a reality? Was it hiring that coaching group? Was it sending in all those applications? Was it coming up with a juicy idea for my talk?

It was none of those. The critical piece to that success was the moment I actually *believed* it was possible.

THE LIFE CHANGE FORMULA: BELIEVE, THINK, FEEL, DO

My TEDx talk would never have become a reality if I first didn't truly believe that it could and would happen. Remember how in the last chapter we discovered that everything is created twice, first in the mind and then in reality? Here is how that works.

True life change isn't random. There is a formula. It's a simple four-step formula, but the amazing thing is that you really only need to focus on the first step—the rest usually takes care of itself. Here's the formula: what you *believe* affects your *thoughts*, which changes how you *feel*, which in turn affects what you *do* each day.

Believe. Think. Feel. Do. And in that order!

I've heard it said that we should do the action and the feeling will come later, and that can be true in some ways. For example, if you're stressed or upset, force yourself to smile for a whole minute and you can definitely change your mood! But that kind of "changing of your state" is only effective for a little while. For long-lasting results, we need to start with our beliefs, and reinforce the ones that will lead to the tangible results we want to see in our lives.

Again, what you believe will determine what you think about. What you think about affects how you feel. And your feelings will lead to your actions. The Irish minister and author Joseph Murphy said it this way in his book *The Power of Your Subconscious Mind*: "As within, so without, meaning according to the image impressed on your subconscious mind, so it is on the objective screen of your life. The outside mirrors the inside. External action follows internal action."

The apostle Paul puts it this way in the book of Romans: "Do not conform to the pattern of this world, but be transformed by the renewing of your mind" (Romans 12:2 NIV). Escaping conformity and transforming your life all begins with renewing. The Greek word for "renewing" there is *anakainōsis*, which means "renovation" or "complete change for the better." You need to renovate the inside of your mind for the outside of your life to be transformed.

And this renewal of your mind isn't a onetime event. It's a way of life. Belief doesn't happen only in an instant, but is an ongoing reality.

That's why it's important to not simply read a book like this, nod your head, and say, "Sure, Graham, I'm going to believe something different right now." Whatever life change you want to see materialize you must daily renew in your mind. Paul says it this way: "Fix your thoughts on what is true, and honorable, and right, and pure, and lovely, and admirable. Think about things that are excellent and worthy of praise. Keep putting into practice all you learned and received from me" (Philippians 4:8–9a NLT). The idea is to daily practice belief, then your thoughts will change, which will overhaul your feelings, which will lead to new actions.

Right belief leads to right thoughts, which lead to right feelings, which lead to right action. And ultimately the result of this formula is the right result!

What I want to do next is show you very practically how to implement this life-change formula in your day-to-day rhythms. It all comes down to two words: prime and protect.

PRIME AND PROTECT YOUR DAY

Back in chapter three, we took a thirty-thousand-foot view of your dreams, desires, and goals for life. Then in chapter four we dialed in a much more specific and clear vision for one of those big dreams. We gave language and detail to it. And in the previous chapter we identified and cleared out the negative mindsets and mental scripts that will keep your dream from happening. So how do we now take massive action on this dream and bring it to fruition? Daily. That's how.

Your dream (and more importantly your authentic life) is created one day at a time. The reality is that all you can focus on is today. This might sound obvious but it's important, simply because of the fact that the only day that actually exists in physical form is today. Yesterday exists in your memories, and tomorrow exists in your mind, but today exists in the present physical four dimensions of time and space.

That being said, the way we implement Step 4 of the REBEL framework, engage in rebellious new thoughts, is on a daily basis. And from this moment forward I want you to do two things each day: prime your day and protect your day. Let's start with priming your day.

Much like priming the pump for an engine gets the fuel in place and ready to go for ignition, priming your day is essential to igniting your life. In short, how you start your day matters. And if you think about it, the start of the day is the only part of the day you can really control. Starting it off well will set the stage for your mind, body, and soul.

I submit to you that the most rebellious thing you can do is to control how you start your day—otherwise, the day will take you where it wants to. *No es bueno.*

Most people start their day by picking up their phone and scrolling through social media, email, or the news. Then it's off to take care of the kids or run out the door to work or school. Within minutes of opening their eyes, most people have been swept up in the current of the day and have already lost the battle. My suggestion is to wait to jump into your day after you've had some priming time (or prime time if you prefer). You will go into the day with peace, power, and purpose rather than letting the current of conformity sweep you up and away from your goals.

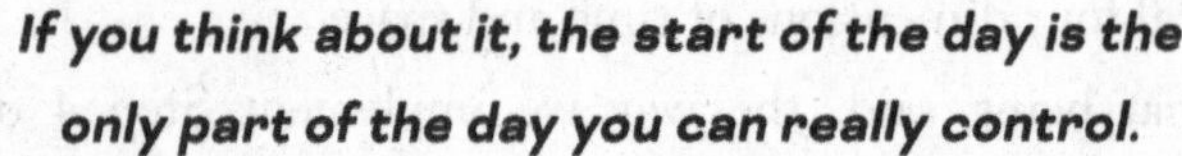

If you think about it, the start of the day is the only part of the day you can really control.

The W.A.I.T. Morning Method (Four Things I Do Every Morning)

In order to prime your day I suggest you create a morning routine of at least thirty minutes that includes the following four things. They are easy to remember because they spell the word WAIT, which is a good reminder to wait to jump into your day until after priming it.

1. **Wisdom.** I believe that the most valuable thing you could acquire in life is wisdom. King Solomon wrote three thousand years ago: "For wisdom is more profitable than silver, and her wages are better than gold. Wisdom is more precious than rubies; nothing you desire can compare with her. She offers you long life in her right hand, and riches and honor in her left. She will guide you down delightful paths; all her ways are satisfying. Wisdom is a tree of life to those who embrace her; happy are those who hold her tightly" (Proverbs 3:14–18 NLT).

Instead of the first thing you put into your mind being the chaos and shallowness of the world, starting your day with a healthy dose of wisdom sets you on a better path as you step out into the world. As a Christian I read the Bible each morning. Whether or not you are a Christian, I'd recommend you read it as well. There is a reason it is the most read and bestselling book of all time. It has benefited its readers for thousands of years.

But even if you choose to read something else, choose something ancient, timeless, and tested. If it's lasted hundreds and thousands of years, there's likely a reason. Ancient wisdom has a way of pulling you out of the myopic modern way of thinking that clearly isn't leading to much happiness and joy for most people.

2. **Affirmation.** After reading some wisdom, I recommend writing down and reviewing what is true and what you *want* to be true in your life—that is your vision. Remember, life change doesn't come from wishful thinking or saying to yourself, "I hope this happens." That's not what affirmations are. Affirmations are the reinforcement of your faith and belief that your dream is inevitable. It will happen.

   The book of Hebrews puts it this way: "Faith is the confidence that what we hope for will actually happen; it gives us assurance about things we cannot see" (Hebrews 11:1 NLT). Some other English translations say that faith is the "substance" of things hoped for. It is solid and very much real.

It's easy to get discouraged and distracted when it comes to creating the life that you want so it's imperative that you review and remind yourself daily of the vision you've written down and committed to making a reality. For months one of my affirmations was, "I am a TEDx speaker and my talk has reached one million people." Part of that affirmation has come true and I have no doubt that the other part will as well. Many times, my affirmations simply state the type of man I choose to become. Recent examples include: "I am confident, calm, and flexible," and "I am content and have everything I need."

3. **Imagination.** Next comes one of my favorite parts. After downloading some timeless wisdom and reviewing your vision through affirmations comes using your imagination. Remember, your vision hasn't become a present reality yet. So one of the powerful things you can do is pre-experience your dream or vision, thereby making it more real to you in your mind and solidifying your belief. Albert Einstein said: "Imagination is more important than knowledge. For knowledge is limited to all we now know and understand, while imagination embraces the entire world, and all there ever will be to know and understand."

Here's what I do and recommend: Spend five minutes in silence imagining and visualizing either your day or an element of your long-term vision—the fit body you will have, the successful business growth you are moving toward, that promotion that is coming your way. Picture specific scenes or moments, complete with colors, sounds, textures, and smells. This might seem awkward at first, but after a few attempts it will get easier, and eventually I believe it will become your favorite time of the day!

One crazy note on imagination and visualization—studies have shown that the mind cannot differentiate between a real or imagined experience. For example, Olympic athletes have been hooked up to sophisticated biofeedback equipment and asked to run their event only in their mind. Amazingly, the same muscles fired in the same sequence when they were running the race in their mind as when they were running it on the track.

Also, golfers have improved their golf swing and basketball players have improved their free throw accuracy simply by "practicing" in their minds. Again, these imagination sessions serve as "experiences" to the mind and reinforce beliefs and confidence, all with your eyes closed. And if it can work for athletes, I think we should take note and apply it to our own dreams as well!

4. **Thankfulness.** Finally, it's important to end your priming time with gratitude. Being thankful is a powerful way of life. And while all of us are likely grateful for many things in our lives if we stop and think about it, the reality is we rarely do just that: stop and think about it. But the benefits are significant!

    Keeping a gratitude journal (i.e., writing down what you are thankful for) has been proven to lead to less stress, improved sleep, more energy and vitality, and overall better mood. This is because gratitude releases both dopamine and serotonin, which make us feel incredible. Gratitude even increases the amount of gray matter in your brain, which is responsible for processing information!

    So my suggestion is simple: write down and reflect on five things you are thankful for each morning. This can take only a handful of seconds or you could combine gratitude and imagination and spend some time "marinating" on something or someone you are grateful for as a mental image.

So there you have it. Prime your day with the simple WAIT Morning Method: Wisdom, Affirmation, Imagination, and Thankfulness. You can do them in that order or rearrange the components however you see fit. Just make sure to wake up at least thirty minutes earlier each day to make this time a priority.

WHAT TO DO WHEN THE DAY GETS AWAY FROM YOU

Most people can get behind the idea of an intentional morning routine to prime your day. A strong start is everything. But what happens as the day goes on and shots are fired, circumstances don't go your way, or you slip into a bad mood? Things that can sound good in a book like this rarely work out perfectly in the real world. So what do you do when reality smacks you in the face by lunchtime?

In short, how you respond matters. You can either protect your day or give up and flow with the negative current of conformity. Remember, that current is always trying to pull you down. It is always flowing in the direction of average, and average these days is depressing. To be a rebel when your day doesn't go your way, you're going to have to fight to protect what you've built. Here are three ways that work well for me.

Set Up Stones of Remembrance

As smart, clever, and creative as we humans are, we also tend to be forgetful. One minute we feel confident about our finances because we've gotten on track and have a plan, but moments later a bill shows up in the mail that we didn't expect and we crumble in an instant. What happened? We forgot the reality that we are really in a good place financially because of the most recent events in our day.

We tend to overemphasize the recent at the expense of reality. We also tend to overweight the negative rather than the positive. The solution? Stones of remembrance.

In the book of Joshua in the Bible, God takes the Israelites across the Jordan River into the Promised Land. He performs a Moses-type miracle and parts the waters so the people can walk across on dry land. It's a really big moment, not just because of the supernatural experience but because of what it symbolizes: God's people have finally entered the land that was promised to them five hundred years earlier.

But God knows that his people will forget this incredible moment. They will encounter scary, dangerous, and frustrating situations in the coming years (even in the Promised Land!). So what does He do? He tells them to grab twelve stones from the river they crossed and set them up as a memorial. He explains:

"We will use these stones to build a memorial. In the future your children will ask you, 'What do these stones mean?' Then you can tell them, 'They remind us that the Jordan River stopped flowing when the Ark of the Lord's Covenant went across.' These stones will stand as a memorial among the people of Israel forever" (Joshua 4:6–7 NLT).

Why do I tell you this story? Because that's exactly what you and I need to do. We need to set up our *own* stones of remembrance, physical items that can act as a visual cue or reminder of where we've come from and where we are headed. Good examples of modern-day stones of remembrance include:

- Vision boards on your wall near where you work
- Journal filled with your dreams and affirmations
- Powerful quotes or memories displayed on your desk, fridge, or bathroom mirror

Pretty much anything visual that is near you will work. The goal is to have prepared in advance for the moment that you get discouraged (and you will) so that your eyes can't help but notice this item or "memorial" and be reminded of your vision.

The Five-Minute Refresh

Sometimes you just need to give yourself a "time-out." Not as a punishment like when we were kids, but as an opportunity to reset and refresh your mind. This one is pretty simple and it works wonders.

First, find a quiet place in your house, your office, or outside. You need to be away from people in a distraction-free environment for just a few minutes. Put your phone in "Do Not Disturb" mode so no one can interrupt you from afar. And finally, set your phone's timer for five minutes. Here's what you do during those few minutes:

- **Do five rounds of box breathing.** Close your eyes, quiet your mind, and begin to picture an imaginary box in front of you. Breathe in through your nose slowly for a four-count, imagining your finger tracing the left side of the box going up. Hold your breath in for a slow four-count as you trace the imaginary box across the top to the right. Then exhale through the mouth for another four-count as you trace the right side of the box down. Finally, hold your empty lungs for a slow four-count as you trace the bottom side of the box across to the left. Repeat this breathing cycle four more times for a total of five rounds. This will help reset your sympathetic nervous system and calm you down.

- **Name five things you're grateful for.** Do a quick gratitude check by thinking of five things you are grateful for. Acknowledge each one quietly in your mind and linger on each for five to ten seconds as you soak in your appreciation for it.
- **Finish with visualization.** Spend the remaining time of your five minutes quietly visualizing one of your dreams. Imagine it going well, picturing it in as much vivid detail as possible. Perhaps it's playing out a certain conversation with someone, or accomplishing a goal. It can even be pre-experiencing that dream vacation that's coming up. Whatever is part of your incredible future, practice enjoying it in your mind now. This is a powerful mood changer.

When the timer goes off, you are done and can open your eyes. What you will have just done is taken back control of your body (through breathing), your heart (through gratitude), and your mind (through visualization)—all in five minutes!

Your Virtual Board of Advisors

Here is one more way to protect your day when things go south. If you find yourself at an impasse with a very specific challenge or situation, it can be incredibly powerful to tap into your virtual board of advisors. My friend and coach Mike Zeller taught me this powerful exercise and it's incredibly useful.

The concept is simple: mentorship and counsel are critical tools in life. We never have all the answers. We all need guidance from time to time. King Solomon, one of the wisest people in recorded history, said, "Where there is no guidance, a people falls, but in an abundance of counselors there is safety" (Proverbs 11:14 ESV).

Just like big, publicly traded companies have a board of advisors (people from outside the company who can weigh in on different issues), you and I should have one too. But ours doesn't have to be limited to people we know, or even people who are still alive! We can create a virtual board of advisors in our minds. Here is how this works:

- **List five to seven people (alive or dead) who you admire and would want to have as a mentor or advisor in your life.** Mine includes authors of books that have impacted my life, great thought leaders of our day, and even Jesus Christ.

- **In one sentence next to each name, list why you would want them on your life's board of advisors.** For example, many of the people on my "board" are there because they have achieved something at a high level in an area I'm trying to break into, but they've also done it while staying married and not compromising their character.
- **Now spend five minutes in a quiet place imagining sitting with them in a conference room (or somewhere more inspiring like a beautiful dinner table or hotel lobby).** Visualize where each of them is sitting in the room, and then present your challenge or question to the group. One by one go down the line imagining how they would respond to you. What advice do you imagine they would give?

A quick example of how I've used this exercise involves this book! I was midway through the writing process and was getting discouraged about my progress. I felt insecure and unsure about the direction I was taking the book. So I created my "virtual board of advisors" and did this exercise mid–writing session. It was amazing how, as I went down the line of individuals in this imaginary board meeting, I instantly received powerful, clear, and helpful advice from each person. When I opened my eyes I knew exactly what I needed to do next with the book and regained my confidence and clarity!

Once you have created your virtual board of advisors you can take a break at any moment you find yourself stuck or in need of counsel and "hold a meeting" in your mind. The reason this works is because it forces you to think about your situation from someone else's perspective. You are literally creating new neural pathways in your brain and this not only snaps you out of a funk or discouraging mood, but can create new insights you didn't previously have.

GOAL FUNNELS (FROM DREAMS TO REALITY)

Remember the life change formula we discussed a few pages ago? Believe. Think. Feel. Do. That is the order and the flow of how real results are created. They begin with your beliefs. This is why we've spent so much time talking about your thoughts, priming your day, and protecting it when circumstances blow you off course. But nothing changes in our lives until we *do* something. Let's talk about that.

The best way I've discovered to achieve your goals and get real results in your life is through something I call goal funnels. You see, as wonderful as they are, there are three core problems with having big goals or dreams:

- They can be overwhelming.
- There is no clear path to achievement.
- They pull you out of your comfort zone.

These reasons (among many others) are why most people never reach their goals or realize their dreams. But not you. We haven't come this far only to talk about dreams and work on our mindset. We've come here to engage in rebellious behavior, to take actions that will lead us to the results we want!

The key is to not get overwhelmed and overly focused on the end result. The great painter Vincent van Gogh said it best: "Great things are done by a series of small things brought together." That's all any major dream or accomplishment is: the result of a series of small things brought together. Goal funnels are the solution. They work because they:

- Fit your actual life/schedule
- Show you what to do each day
- Make achieving your goals inevitable

Imagine a funnel or cone shape. It has three main sections: the top section or opening (which is the widest point), the middle section (which gets a bit narrower), and the bottom section (which is so small it comes to a point). The way I like to achieve any big dream or goal is to break it down into three parts, like the funnel. Here's how this works. Pull out your journal or notes app and create three sections on the page: the top, middle, and bottom of the funnel.

1. **Top of the goal funnel.** At the top, write down what your biggest goal or dream is that you want to see realized in the next twelve months of your life. This can be one simple sentence or a short paragraph. Next, write down why that dream or goal is that important to you and worth pursuing over the next year.

   An example might be: "I want to get a promotion at my job in the next twelve months. I want this because I want to improve my lifestyle for my family. Specifically, I want to use the extra money to pay off my student loans and put a down payment on a house."
2. **Mid level of goal funnel.** In the next section as we go down the funnel, you want to answer the question: *What would have to happen to achieve that top-level goal?* You likely know this intuitively. But even if you don't, this is where you can begin to do some basic research or seek counsel from someone who has achieved this same goal before. The idea here is to pinpoint the core activities that drive results.

   Going back to our example. If our top of the funnel goal is to get a promotion and subsequent pay raise in the next twelve months, then our mid-level activities might look like: talk to my boss and find out what her biggest challenges are coming up, talk to my coworkers and find out where they could use some help, find the top salesperson (if you're in sales) or someone who already has the position you want and take them out to coffee to find out what it takes to get there.

3. **Bottom level of goal funnel.** Finally, we arrive at the bottom of the funnel, the smallest part. This is where we answer the question: *What should my days look like to make all the above mid-level activities happen?* This is where the rubber meets the road, as they say, and we go from just a dream or goal to daily habits and choices (the series of small things van Gogh talks about) that add up to major life change.

   An example of what I might write down for our job promotion goal would be: come in to work thirty minutes early and stay thirty minutes late every day, take one thing off of a coworker's plate each week, each month ask my boss for an additional project to take on without any additional pay and spend a few minutes each day working on it, do an 80/20 analysis of my work tasks and decipher what 20 percent of my activity is leading to 80 percent of my results and double down on that, and read one leadership book per month.

Here's the amazing thing. In this example, if you were to follow this plan, one year from now your reputation in your company would be completely transformed for the better and yet all you did were these tiny, boring, incremental steps on a day-to-day basis. Your dream was first created in your mind but it's created in the physical world by your daily decisions.

Your dream is made up of tiny actions, but you will only pursue actions if you believe they lead to the dream you wish to see become a reality. As bestselling author James Clear says in his book *Atomic Habits*, "Every action you take is a vote for the person you wish to become."

JUST TAKE THE NEXT STEP

One final note of encouragement here. Some goals or dreams don't have as many obvious daily steps to take to make them a reality. Sometimes you don't know what you are doing and it can feel incredibly discouraging. May I remind you that you don't need to know the entire map of how your dream or vision is coming true. You just need to focus on the next step.

For example, when I got serious about my dream to write my first book, *How to Get Paid for What You Know*, I knew absolutely nothing about writing a book and getting it published. All I had was my dream and belief that I could be a bestselling author, which created new thoughts and feelings, which led to my decision to take action on making my first book a reality. But where should I start?

The only step I knew to take was to buy that course from bestselling author Michael Hyatt on how to get published. It was a logical step because I saw some emails from him promoting the course, so I purchased it and watched it all the way through. Then I asked myself: Do I know any bestselling authors personally who I could talk to and get advice from? Turns out I did! I reached out to my friend Jordan Raynor and in one phone call I learned a ton about the process. Which led to my next step of ideating my book idea, which led to my next step of creating a book proposal, and so on.

My point is that, in hindsight, my author journey looks nice and linear. I had a dream to write and publish a book. Two years later it became a reality. In truth, though, I had no idea which path to follow. All I did was take the next step, and then the next step, which eventually led to yet another step. But one step at a time is enough to get you anywhere you want to go.

Remember, you can successfully drive cross country from Los Angeles to New York City (a 2,800-mile trip) in the dark with headlights that only illuminate the next two hundred feet in front of you.

In the next chapter we will discuss the final step in the REBEL framework—letting go of what others think of you (including what you think of *yourself*) as you start living the Rebel Lifestyle. Spoiler alert: it's a lot messier than I'd like to admit, but it's worth it!

The Final Hurdles to Living the Rebel Lifestyle

Step 5: Let Go of Outcomes and Others' Opinions

In the early 1990s, a brilliant young Princeton University graduate quit his cushy, multi-six-figure-a-year job on Wall Street to open a bookstore . . . on the internet. His name was Jeff Bezos and the "store" was called Amazon.com.

We know how the story ends. Bezos became a billionaire (many years, his wealth ranks him as the richest person on the planet) and his vision for Amazon has grown to a $500-billion-plus-a-year business and the fifth-most-visited website in America every day. What began as a way to buy and sell books online in an era when nobody did that has turned into one of the largest places to buy just about anything you could ever want.

Clearly, we would all agree that starting Amazon was a great move. But thirty years ago, everybody tried to talk Bezos out of the idea.

Bezos's Wall Street boss loved him and even supported his idea to start Amazon but thought it was foolish to quit his job entirely. When Bezos called his parents and told them he was quitting and starting Amazon, their response was: "What do you mean, you are going to sell books over the internet?" His mom, Jackie, even suggested to her son that he run this new company at night or on the weekends (the "safe" route). Even Bezos himself thought it might be foolish to do what he was doing.

However, one thing Bezos is famous for is his regret minimization framework. When making tough decisions he tries to project himself decades into the future and assess his decision based on how much regret he would have with either choice. In the end, Bezos realized he had to live free of regret and pursue his dream of launching Amazon. In his own words, as detailed in the book *The Everything Store* by Brad Stone:

> When you are in the thick of things, you can get confused by the small stuff. I knew when I was eighty that I would never, for example, think about why I walked away from my 1994 Wall Street bonus in the middle of the year at the worst possible time. That kind of thing just isn't something you worry about when you are eighty years old. At the same time, I knew that I might sincerely regret not having participated in this thing called the Internet that I thought was going to be a revolutionizing event. When I thought about it in that way . . . it was incredibly easy to make the decision.

Keep in mind that when Bezos made the scary decision to quit his job, be a rebel, and go all in on his dream, Amazon was not even close to the complete vision he had for it. The original concept for Amazon was what Bezos called "the everything store," an unlimited storefront where you could buy anything you could want online. That is what Amazon is today, but it wasn't possible to pull off back in 1994.

So Bezos started with the one part of his vision that *was* possible back then: selling books. It was the easiest item to sell online at the time so he began there. This "limitation" didn't stop him from pursuing his dream, it only dictated *how* he would start. The rest, as they say, is history.

Whether you like Amazon and Jeff Bezos or not, the moral of the story is powerful:

Your dreams and your authentic life won't be made manifest if you don't have the guts to be a rebel, even when it's messy, and especially when others you love and respect think you're foolish.

If the first four steps of the REBEL framework are the "What" being a rebel looks like, this fifth and final step is the "How" to live out being a rebel in the real world. Specifically in this chapter we need to address how to live free, and in three ways: live free from perfectionism, live free from outcomes, and live free from other people's opinions.

THE REBEL LIFE IS MESSY (AND THAT'S OK)

To live free in life you must let go of the illusion of perfectionism. Perfect doesn't exist, so if you are chasing it, you'll constantly come up short and be disappointed. Real life is messy and living the rebel life is no exception. Sometimes it won't go well. Other times reaching what you're striving for will take longer than you'd hoped. Still other times you will feel stupid or awkward along the journey.

Speaking of feeling stupid, one of my favorite lines in one of my favorite books, *The Go-Giver* by Bob Burg and John David Mann, goes like this: "Sometimes the thing feels foolish, but you do it anyway."

Much of what we do in life that leads to greatness feels foolish along the way.

Whether it's judgment from outsiders (more on that in a minute) or just the inevitable frustrating bumps along the path, living a life of purpose and intentionality can feel silly at times. But that doesn't mean it's not working or worth pursuing.

In 2018, my wife, Shay, and I decided it was time to try something we had dreamed of for a long time: living in another country for a month. I love the area of Provence in the South of France (and speak a little bit of French myself) so we announced to our kids that 2018 was going to be the summer of France. We booked flights, Airbnbs, and blocked off all work for the month of July.

When you look at the pictures on Instagram or our photo album, we look super happy. Because we were. And when I tell people that we took a month away from our businesses and lived in another country with two young kids, they are impressed. Because it is rare and impressive.

And yet it was equally a hot mess. We almost missed a cross-country train because I couldn't figure out what track our train was supposed to be on and my French language skills were failing me as my stress levels rose. We got stuck in a parking garage because the machine wouldn't take my credit card and I didn't have any more cash. And most of the time my daughters complained that they were bored out of their minds and just wished they were back home with their toys and their friends. These were the inevitable downsides of living internationally for a month. But I'd make that trade again in a heartbeat. You can't have your dream without some form of mess, frustration, or confusion.

Another rebel decision we made years ago was to have family dinner together around the table (with no technology!) every night of the week. Granted, some nights there is an event where one or two of us has to be somewhere else, but we've committed to making family dinner together the rule rather than the exception. And what a powerful rule it is. Parents, I would argue that if you could only do one thing to completely change your family for the better it would be to fight for family dinner together every night and rearrange your life around that.

And yet, it's hard to fight for. As my girls get older, they have more activities and interests outside the home that make having dinner together a challenge. It would be easier to give in and give up on this daily ritual, but we believe even if it's messy and we have to eat at different times each night, it's something worth fighting for.

The same is true with my marriage. As of this writing, Shay and I have been married eighteen years, we are best friends, and are still in love with each other! But if I'm honest, some days I just want to give up. And I'm sure Shay does as well. In this day and age, staying married to someone your entire life is a rebellious move. It takes effort, and sometimes you don't feel like your efforts are making a difference, but they are. That's how you stay married for eighteen years—you "keep doing the thing" even if it seems foolish.

Other examples of how we are choosing to live the rebel life even if it's messy:

- **We refused to get our daughter Chloe a cell phone until she was thirteen, even though most of her friends had one since they were nine or ten.** And even now at fourteen, her phone doesn't have full internet access or any social media apps. You might be able to imagine all the pushback we've gotten from her over the years, especially since most of her friends' parents don't hold our same beliefs around technology. It's been messy—but worth it.
- **I upset customers and clients when I take extended time off with my family.** Most people are cool with it, but inevitably when I take two to four weeks off to travel and unplug from work (I literally do not check email or dive into my community), someone is upset at me. And that means that some people cancel my coaching programs or think I don't care about

them and tell others as much. That hurts my heart (I'm a people pleaser) but it's just part of the process of living the rebel life.

- **We give away 50 percent of our income each month, which is sometimes complicated.** In my TEDx talk, "Why Givers Are Happier and Have Less Money Stress," I outlined our giving journey from being on food stamps to reaching millions a year in income and how our dream was always to eventually give half of what we make away. Now that we are doing that, the reality is that sometimes it's scary to give that much away. And there's a burden of responsibility to make sure that the recipients of each financial gift (whether our church, a nonprofit helping alleviate child poverty like Compassion International, or simply a single mother who can't pay her rent this month) are going to steward that money wisely. It's messy, but still worth doing.

Whatever steps you choose to take on your Rebel Journey and whatever dreams you choose to pursue, it won't be perfect. Likely not even close. In fact, at times you may feel like you are not even making any progress, but trust me, you are. Simply the decision to rebel in an area of your life is in itself progress. Remember, sometimes the thing feels foolish, but you do it anyway.

LOVE THE PROCESS AND YOU'LL LOVE THE OUTCOME

I love personality tests and I've taken quite a few of them over the years. Not surprisingly, with each personality test I take, a pattern seems to emerge: I am future-outcome oriented. For example, my number one strength on the StrengthsFinder assessment is "Futuristic." I'm a 3 on the Enneagram, which is the "Achiever" (also one of my top five strengths on StrengthsFinder).

In summary, I like results. I live for the outcome. It's why I do anything I do.

But there is a double whammy dark side of living for the outcome. First, you aren't satisfied until you reach the outcome. This is a nonstarter. Some outcomes and dreams take ten to twenty years to achieve. Do you really want to live an unsatisfied life for the next decade or two until you reach that specific outcome? I sure don't.

The second dark side is that once you *do* reach that dream outcome, the achievement-induced dopamine hit wears off (sometimes in as little as twenty-four hours) and then you're right back to where you were (being unsatisfied) and must find a new outcome to create or specific result to pursue. Talk about a vicious and depressing cycle!

I can get frustrated when I see my vision or dream so clearly and believe with all my heart that it can and will become reality, but it's just not happening at the pace or in the way that I want. This can lead me into days of feeling discouraged, insecure, confused, and in general having a low state of mind. But it doesn't have to be this way.

My friend and bestselling author Jon Gordon has this great quote: "If you love the process you will love what the process produces."

There is so much wisdom and beauty in that one sentence. Love is a choice. You and I are free to start loving the process of pursuing our dreams and living life by design at any point we choose. Joy is also a choice. At any point in time we can choose to enjoy the journey we are on, even if the outcome hasn't been reached yet.

By choosing to focus on the process of being a rebel and chasing your dreams and choosing to *love* and *enjoy* that process, you unlock two powerful benefits:

1. **You remove the pressure or burden of the outcome.** It's like literally taking off a weighted vest or jacket. You no longer are worried about the outcome. You can still envision the outcome, affirm the outcome, pray for the outcome, but you no longer have the pressure to "make it happen." You are committed to the process and trusting that the rest will take care of itself.
2. **You get to enjoy life *now* and not in some distant future.** Tomorrow is not guaranteed, so why

put off joy until an unpromised date down the road? Choose to love the process and the journey that you are on *today*! This, right now, is your actual life. Too many of us are living what author Sandra Anne Taylor calls the layover mentality. In her book *Quantum Success*, she writes:

> Oftentimes, we don't have any desire to stay in the present because we simply don't think that it's special enough to be worth our full attention. This approach is just filling time while waiting for something better to come along. We see our lives as an endless series of mediocre and mundane activities sprinkled with only a few truly happy or special events. And while we're waiting for those red-letter days to come along, we live with boredom and disinterest in what's going on around us—or perhaps even resentment or disgust.
>
> This is what I call a layover mentality: deciding that everyday life doesn't warrant enthusiasm or happiness. We're merely on a layover, waiting for some special, but all-too-fleeting, event to lift us temporarily out of our doldrums. This moment isn't just a meaningless layover on the way to something else, it's an actual destination in and of itself!

So choosing to love the process removes the burden of achieving the outcome and allows you to enjoy your life along the way *to* the outcome. But there's actually one more hidden benefit to living this way. Ironically, those who love their lives and what they are doing each day create incredible things and build beautifully fulfilling lives.

In short, when you love the process, you'll create beautiful outcomes. Loving the process is the method to achieving the outcomes you want!

A good example of this was the process of writing this book.

When God gave me the idea for this book, I was so excited. I knew it would help millions of people (myself included!) and I couldn't wait to write it and put it out in the world. But then I got so fixated on the outcome (a successful book launch and people loving the book) that I felt a ton of pressure to write something truly worthy of that dream. That pressure that bubbled up in me literally stole the joy out of the experience for about six weeks. I had writer's block, was burdened by deep insecurity and fear, and began to resent the book.

After having some conversations with Jon Gordon as well as implementing the virtual board of advisors exercise I shared with you in chapter six, I got unstuck, saw things clearly, and let go of the pressure. Consequently, the rest of the book came faster, more effortlessly, and was the most fun I've had writing or creating something in a long time!

I know you want your specific goals, dreams, and visions to materialize; otherwise, why would you care about them? And I get the irony that Step 2 of the REBEL framework is to establish the outcomes you want for your life and here in Step 5 I'm telling you to let go of those outcomes. This is not a contradiction but rather a nuance. In order to create amazing results in our lives, we must *both* get clear on the outcomes we desire while at the same time holding those outcomes loosely and focusing more on the process that will create those outcomes.

For example, one of my dream outcomes is to become a *New York Times* bestselling author. I have established that as part of my vision. However, what I'm focused on is not the actual outcome but the process. I ask myself this question: Who do I need to become and what actions do I need to take in order to be a *New York Times* bestselling author? Again, by focusing on who I need to become in order to achieve my desired outcome rather than the outcome itself, I will be more likely to achieve that outcome. So please believe me when I say that the real secret to being a rebel is to love the process and enjoy the journey, every step of the way. Anything short of that is doing yourself a disservice.

CREATE YOUR OWN VALUES (AND LIVE BY THEM)

One reason many people live in bondage is that they feel they are falling short of other people's expectations of them. They care too much about what other people think of them.

Dear friend, you can never truly be free if you are trying to live up to someone else's standards. And the reason is simple: those standards were never meant for you!

They were based on someone else's life, dreams, and values. One final and powerful step you can take in this Rebel Journey that will bring you peace and freedom along the way is to live *your* values and not someone else's values.

We all value different things in life. This is an intuitive process. But let me ask you: Have you ever stopped to articulate and create a list of life or family values that are meaningful and true to you? Because once you do, you will be free from other people's opinions and other people's standards. You will be able to hold yourself accountable to something *you* put in place and believe is important to your life.

I remember the first time we did this as a family. It was the summer of 2019 and we were on vacation in the Rocky Mountains of Colorado. We rented this beautiful house on the top of a mountain and most days before or after a hike Shay and I would sit outside on one of the decks and read, talk, pray, and dream.

One day we had a conversation about our family values. We had never written any of them down, even though we were living them already. We decided to get clear on what it was that we, the Cochrane family, truly valued in life so that we could have a document (i.e., my notes app on my iPhone) to remind us. Here are the five family values we came up with that beautiful June day:

- **Generosity** (doing it, modeling it, encouraging it)
- **Hospitality** (hosting, offering a peaceful place to stay/visit, nice food and drink)
- **Leader/Influencer for Jesus** (being pro-marriage, -family, -faith, -generosity, –financial stewardship, -humility)
- **Creativity/Support for the Arts** (seeing shows, going to museums, playing music, drawing, painting, photography)
- **Entrepreneurship** (supporting an entrepreneurial spirit in our kids and others, having a family "bank" we can use as capital to support ideas)

This isn't an exhaustive list of what we value as a family or individuals, but they are five core values that we've already been living and are somewhat unique to us. They perfectly align with our gifts, passions, and opportunities to serve others.

For example, both the value of Entrepreneurship and Leader/ Influencer for Jesus come from the fact that both Shay and I have businesses and very public content and online audiences. We love being business owners and having the ability to create wealth and the freedom to work when and where we want. This is important to us so that our children see that you can serve the world and build a great life for yourself by being an entrepreneur.

Also, we are naturally leading people and we are intentionally trying to elevate Christian principles, ethics, and teachings in the world because we believe God knows how life works best and His ways will bring the most love, joy, and peace into the world.

Creativity and Support for the Arts comes from our love of theater, music, dance, and visual arts. Each of us in my family has creative talents so we love both to create our own art and enjoy others' as well. We intend to keep creating art ourselves while also supporting local artists and productions in our city.

Generosity and Hospitality go hand in hand for us as we believe everything we have is a gift from God and is meant to be shared with others. Our home is a great place for us to live, but it is also a wonderful opportunity to love on others by inviting them over and blessing them with a great meal, conversation, and care. Our money is also meant to be shared with those who need it even more than we do. We view ourselves as a conduit of God's resources, not a reservoir. Money flows through us, not just to us.

Hopefully this gives you a bit of context of how family values can work. We have agreed, together as a family, that these five things matter to us and we try to make decisions and live life in a way that honors and reflects those values.

TWO QUESTIONS YOU SHOULD ASK YOURSELF

Now it's time to create your *own* set of personal or family values. If you are getting stuck, I'd suggest you create a value for each of the six main categories of life we covered in chapter two. If you don't remember, they are: work, time, finances, relationships, health, and spirituality.

On a blank piece of paper (or in your notes app or Google doc) write down the words "My Family Values" or "My Personal Values." Then list out the six categories I just mentioned. Next to each category, I want you to simply answer these two questions:

- **What is the most important thing to me/us when it comes to [CATEGORY]?**
- **How will I know that I am successful in the area of [CATEGORY]?**

For example, you might start with the finances category and answer the questions this way:

The most important thing to us when it comes to finances is that we are financially free. I will know that we are successful in this area of finances because we will have six months of expenses saved in the bank and we will always spend less than we earn each month.

The point is to force yourself (and your spouse) to articulate what you truly value in each domain of life, both from a macro perspective and from an on-the-ground micro perspective. For example, our family value of hospitality could look very different in your home than in ours. For us it's all about having people over, making them a home-cooked meal, having deep, fun, meaningful conversation, and giving them a quiet, restful place to stay. For you, hospitality might look like bringing meals to sick friends or people in your church who just had a baby.

That's the fun of it. You get to decide what you value and what that looks like specifically in your life.

So take some time right now (or later today with your spouse) to sit down and answer those two questions for each of the six domains of life (work, time, finances, relationships, health, and spirituality). If you already know what your values are but just have never written them down, great! Write them down now. Get clear on them. Edit them until they feel exciting and true to you.

The goal is to have a set of values that really fires you up and feels authentic to who you are as a person and a family unit. Remember, it's pointless to create "values" that you actually don't value!

YOUR REBEL LIFE WILL INSPIRE OTHERS

Let's pause for a moment and look back at what you've accomplished up to this point. So far in your Rebel Journey:

- You've seen that most people are living on autopilot and autopilot living will lead you away from the life you want.
- You have given yourself permission to live differently and dream again.
- You've identified what the tangible outcomes of those dreams look like over the next three years.
- You've done an Inner Story Audit and begun to break old thinking, mental scripts, and habits that are holding you back.
- You are actively thinking new thoughts, priming and protecting your day, and taking active steps toward your vision.
- You've decided on and declared your own set of personal or family values that you will build your life on.

Even if you've just read through this book quickly and intend to do the exercises when you're all done reading, you at least have seen the problem (conformity) and now know the solution (be a rebel) and have the road map to become one (the five-part REBEL framework). Just by holding this book in your hands and going on this journey with me in your mind, you have, in the words of Obi-Wan Kenobi, "taken your first step into a larger world."

But here's the cool thing. That larger world isn't just about you or for you. Yes, your world is about to get larger as the Rebel Lifestyle is all about challenging norms and stepping into your full potential. But that larger, better world is also for those around you. When you live the Rebel Lifestyle you will actually inspire *others* to become rebels as well. People are watching you and many of those people will be impacted and deeply influenced by the way you choose to live your life.

So, as you begin to embrace your uniqueness, get intentional, and create the life you've always wanted to live, you will be paving the way for those around you to come as well. The more you rebel, the more you make it OK for others to rebel as well!

In our next and final chapter, I want to share with you a profound truth about how to find your calling and life purpose!

8

The Surprisingly Simple Way to Find Your Life's Purpose

Author Dan Miller tells this story about a Jewish rabbi who lived in the time of Christ during the height of the Roman Empire. One day he was traveling back home from a long journey to another town and accidentally took a wrong turn without realizing it. He was so caught up with his prayers and inner thoughts that he didn't notice he was far from his intended path for a few hours.

Suddenly he overheard a loud, booming voice that startled him. "Who are you, and why are you here?!" the voice said. The rabbi looked up and realized he was standing in front of the gate of a Roman military outpost, and guarding that gate was a tall, armored Roman centurion. As the rabbi was taking in the fact that he was not at his intended destination and was looking at his surroundings, he did not answer. Again, the centurion questioned him: "Who are you, and why are you here?!"

Then the rabbi looked up at the guard and asked him: "Young man, how much do they pay you to stand guard and ask those questions of those who approach?" Rather than being defensive, the guard could then see that he was dealing with a man of the cloth—not an intruder. He answered, "Four drachmas a week [roughly $100]." The rabbi replied immediately, "I'll double your pay if you come with me, stand at the door of my cabin, and ask me those same two questions each morning as I leave for the day."

I love this story so much because it calls attention in a simple and memorable way to the only two questions that really matter in life: Who are you? And why are you here?

If you can discover the answer to those two questions (and daily remind yourself of the answers), you can operate in the world with confidence, boldness, clarity, and joy—unlike the rest of the world that is desperately confused about their identity and their purpose.

YOUR IDENTITY PRECEDES YOUR DESTINY

You can't know your purpose in life (the "why" you are here) until you know yourself (the "who" you are). So many people want to figure out their life's work or their personal mission and they start there. Simon Sinek even popularized the phrase "Start with Why" with his bestselling book and popular TED talk of the same name. But you really can't start with "Why." You must start with "Who."

My friend and coach Mike Zeller has this saying: "Your identity precedes your destiny." I couldn't agree more. Finding yourself (what this book is all about) gives you so much more clarity as to what to *do* in this world. But as we've discussed, culture can't tell you who you are, your work can't tell you who you are, and even your family can't tell you who you are.

Interestingly, only your Creator can.

Remember my espresso machine from chapter one? That machine can't come up with its own identity or purpose. It has been given one by its creator (the espresso machine company). You and I are the same. The Bible tells us we were made in God's image, which means if we quiet ourselves and look closely inside, we will find clues as to who we truly are.

The REBEL framework you've just worked through helps you uncover who you truly are by forcing you to quiet the outside noise and look inside at what's been in front of you your whole life but you've either forgotten or never noticed:

- In Step 1 you **resolved to dream again** and live differently than the culture around you suggests you should. You started the journey of self-discovery by examining your dreams and desires. Most people never stop to do this. They are too busy chasing the dreams that everyone else seems to have. We do this long enough and we no longer know what *our* dreams and desires look like. And yet our desires are clues as to how God made us and wired us. They are clues to the puzzle of who we are!
- In Step 2 you **established the outcomes** you want for your life. This is where you flexed your creative mind and got specific about what your ideal life looks like even down to the day-to-day rhythms. By crafting a detailed vision for what *your* ideal life looks like, you made it that much more likely to live the life *you*

were called to live and not just slip into the default existence. Again, these specifics didn't come from nowhere; they are residual traces of God's design in your life. Psalm 37:4 (NIV) says, "[God] will give you the desires of your heart." Literally, your desires were put there by God Himself!

- In Step 3 you **broke the old way of thinking** by acknowledging the negative inner story playing out in your mind based on outdated programming. You were not born with that inner story or those unhealthy mental scripts. They were put there by the world and by an enemy who hates you. God made you perfect with a clear mind, so before we can use it to become who we were meant to become, we need to delete the lies we believe so we can more clearly see the truth of how God sees us.
- In Step 4 you **engaged in rebellious new thinking.** With a renewed vigor and clarity, you began to step into who you are with new beliefs, which lead to new thoughts, which lead to new feelings, which lead to new actions, which ultimately lead to new results in your life. Who you are on the inside begins to manifest on the outside as you step into your rediscovered identity.
- And finally, in Step 5, you chose to **let go and live free** from perfectionism, specific outcomes, and other people's opinions. You embraced the messy reality of

living the Rebel Lifestyle and created your own set of personal or family values, which aren't based on what others value but on what *you* value.

If you actually take the time to work through the exercises I created for you in each step of the process, you will have a really good idea of who you are. Congratulate yourself because you are in the top 5 percent of all humans on the planet when it comes to self-reflection and the inner work needed for real growth, joy, and life satisfaction. But it's only scratching the surface of *why* you are here.

YOUR CALLING IS AN EXTENSION OF WHO YOU ARE

It's taken me a long time to figure this out, but your purpose in life isn't what you *do*; it's an overflow of who you *are*.

You will likely have many different jobs, vocations, responsibilities, businesses, and communities that you serve during the course of your life. But none of those are your calling or purpose in and of themselves.

Once you know who you are, what you care about, what dreams light you up, and you begin to live out those dreams and desires, what flows out of living that freely in service of others is your purpose.

And that purpose or calling can change over time. But your identity (who you are) never will.

The beauty of this is that it's an internal work, not an external one. Once you find yourself, you can show up differently in the world you already inhabit, in the job you already inhabit, with the friends and family life you already inhabit. You can begin to live out your unique awesomeness right now, today, without needing to "find your purpose" elsewhere.

It also means that you are free to make a change if what you're doing is not aligned with who you truly are. You are free to be creative and pursue new things and serve new people. By becoming a rebel, you aren't now supposed to follow a prescribed path of rebellion (that would be another version of conformity, and very ironic). Instead, think of it as having become whole again. You are back to who God intended you to be, and now the journey can really begin.

For years I thought my calling was to be a musician. Then I thought my purpose was to be a content creator on YouTube and then a business coach. But as I've done the inner work, I've discovered something profound: my identity (who I am) is an encourager and speaker of life. That's what I love to do! My favorite thing is to pour into people, give them hope, and literally speak words of life into their soul so they walk away feeling valued, inspired, and, more importantly, empowered to do what's in their heart!

Who I am (a speaker of words of life) tells me why I am here (to pour into other people in everything I do). Following my desires and dreams from Step 1 of the REBEL framework, I have enough clues to know that I love making content (videos, podcasts, and books) as well as speaking on stages. I also love travel and working on my own schedule. That means being an author, speaker, and coach is a perfect calling and purpose for me because it flows out of who I truly am and what desires God has put in my heart.

But you know what? If for some reason all of that changes in the future (writing, speaking, coaching), my identity won't change. Who I am at the core will always be the same—my calling will just shift. One day I will be a grandfather and live out my identity as a speaker of words of life as I read books to my grandkids and pour encouragement and belief over their lives. Same identity, new flavor of the calling.

As you find yourself, your calling and purpose will become clearer and clearer around every corner: no matter what season of life you are in. The fun is really just beginning!

THE LIFE PURPOSE MATRIX

With that in mind I want to give you a helpful tool I developed for my clients to begin to discover their life's purpose (or calling). It's called the Life Purpose Matrix and it's both powerful and simple.

Take out a piece of paper and draw a grid of four boxes or a simple cross with four empty quadrants. On the axis going left to right, you'll write the word "values"; and on the axis going bottom to top, you'll write the word "dreams." As with any good 2 x 2 matrix there are four quadrants representing four possible combinations. We're going to fill out each box with activities, tasks, and possible life pursuits.

In the bottom left quadrant, list out the things you are doing (or think you should do) in life that you don't love to do and don't align with your personal values (you created a list of your personal values in chapter seven, remember?). In the top left quadrant, list out things you are doing that you love but don't align with your values. In the bottom right quadrant, list out things you are doing that you don't love but do align with your values. And finally, in the top right quadrant, list out the things you are doing that you love to do that also align with your values. Anything that lands in that top right quadrant is where the gold is. Pursue those things. They will lead you to your life's purpose. The Life Purpose Matrix looks like the diagram on the following page.

Another way to approach the Life Purpose Matrix is to take a task, or job, or potential life pursuit and filter it through all four quadrants. Ask yourself, *Which box does this fit in? Does it line up with what I love to do (my dreams) and what I value as a person or a family member?* If it's missing one or both of those qualifications, it's not life purpose material. If it checks both boxes, you have a green light to move forward in your exploration process!

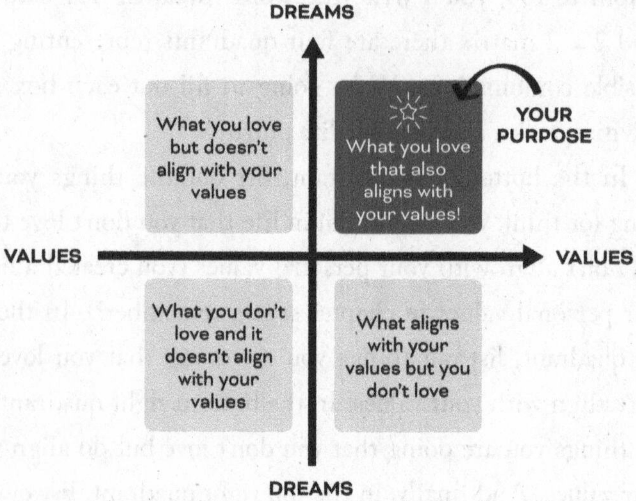

I'll give you an example in my own life and business for all four quadrants of the Life Purpose Matrix. I love traveling and speaking, but I also value being home as much as possible with my family, so I've been very selective about my speaking engagements while I have young kids in the house. That would fall in the top left quadrant for now. Helping record and produce albums for indie artists and bands (what I used to do years ago) lines up with my values of helping people pursue their calling, but I don't love to do it anymore. That would fall in the bottom right quadrant.

But writing bestselling books and hosting a top podcast—both of which help people uncover their uniqueness and create more money, margin, and meaning in their lives—is absolutely something that fits in the top right quadrant and is life purpose material. They are both things I love to do and they line up with my values of serving others and being able to be home and present with my family!

So what about you? Is what you're pursuing right now life purpose material? Where does it plot along the Life Purpose Matrix? Consider noodling on this tool for a while any time you consider a new opportunity that comes your way. In life there will be a plethora of things to pursue—the trick is knowing which ones are the right fit for you. This is why knowing your dreams and your values is so critical to loving your life.

TAKE THE 30-DAY REBEL CHALLENGE

Before we end our brief time together, I want to leave you with one more valuable tool, something that will help you take what you've learned here and apply it in the real world.

You see, the problem with being an author and writing a book like this is that books don't change lives—at least not on their own. Readers like you change their *own* lives when they take massive action on what they read in a book like this. That's why I've already included a handful of powerful action-oriented exercises in the preceding chapters. But I wanted to give you something that would go well beyond the pages of this book, my 30-Day Rebel Challenge. It's absolutely free and it will 100 percent change your life if you take it seriously.

Each day for the next thirty days I will email you with an exercise, a quote, a resource, or some good old-fashioned motivation to keep you going on this journey of finding yourself and making a difference in your world!

Just go to www.grahamcochrane.com/rebelbonus to get instant access to the free 30-Day Rebel Challenge. Also, don't forget to take a picture of you holding your book and tag me in it on Instagram (@thegrahamcochrane) so I can share it with my community and encourage them to join us on this Rebel's Journey!

Also, if you'll allow me, I'd like to make two small but powerful suggestions that will help you on your journey:

- **Find a rebel buddy**—Don't do this alone. Grab a friend, spouse, or family member to go on this journey with you and hold you accountable (buy them a copy of this book!). Applying the REBEL framework and finding yourself is good, deep inner work and it can be easy to give up and slip right back into the current of conformity. Remember, that's the default mode because it's easier. If you have a "rebel buddy," you will be more likely to stick with the process and love the results it creates.
- **Pick ONE dream to focus on**—If you did the fifty dreams exercise in chapter three, then you likely have

a handful of desires you are really excited about bringing to reality. My suggestion is to start with one for now. As that dream becomes more of a reality in the next thirty days, you will be more likely to activate the remaining dreams. If you do too much at once, you will get overwhelmed and quit. And if you quit, nobody wins.

So pick your dream to start with, find a rebel buddy, and then jump into the 30-Day Rebel Challenge. And here's the amazing thing: the ripple effects of what you do over the next thirty days will reach far beyond you. You have no idea just how profound this decision to escape conformity, dream again, and create the life you were meant for truly is.

FIND YOURSELF FOR THE SAKE OF THOSE YOU LOVE

I want to leave you with what may seem like an odd story, but I believe it reveals a critical final truth to this Rebel Journey we've gone on together. Once you understand this piece of the puzzle, life will make a lot more sense for you.

In the book of Mark, in chapter five, there is an account of Jesus healing a demon-possessed man living in a cemetery. This man was so violent and strong that he couldn't be kept chained down to anything, and all the people in the region were scared of him. Add to that the fact that he would walk the graveyard "howling and cutting himself with sharp stones" (Mark 5:5 NLT). Crazy stuff, I know.

After a dramatic scene that reminds me of a horror movie, Jesus calls the evil spirit out of the man and restores him completely to his right mind and self. The moment is so intense that the townspeople actually ask Jesus to leave their area. But guess who *doesn't* want Jesus to leave? The previously demon-possessed man. Specifically, the man wants to journey with Jesus and become one of His followers, but in a response that seems confusing at best and cruel at worst, Jesus doesn't let him. Here's what Jesus says instead:

"No, go home to your family, and tell them everything the Lord has done for you and how merciful he has been" (Mark 5:18–19 NLT).

Why am I telling you this story? Lean in for a moment and you'll see the real reason you were meant to read this book.

This man has just had a profound change in his life, is restored to his true self, and then understandably wants to leave everything, including his old life and world, behind. He feels brand new and so he wants to *go* somewhere brand new and be with brand-new people.

But instead, Jesus tells him to go back home *as* his new self.

Being a rebel isn't always about leaving your old life behind; it's really about bringing your true self into your current life.

The people around you need you to rebel (your spouse, your family, your coworkers, your employees, your community). They need the real you, the joyful you, the confident you, the you that is at peace within yourself.

Because here's the secret: At the end of the day, finding yourself isn't really about you at all. Ultimately, it's about the people you will impact. Your joy becomes their joy, your confidence becomes their confidence, and your peace becomes their peace. You have so much to give the world, but it starts with discovering who you truly are in the first place.

So, friend, once you find yourself, "go back home" and bring this message to those you love and watch what happens next!

READER'S GUIDE

Here you'll find discussion questions and action steps for each chapter in this book. I hope these questions and suggestions will reinforce the central principles, help you stay focused, and inspire you to stay on this Rebel's Journey and do life your way.

CHAPTER 1: THE ONE MENTAL SHIFT THAT CHANGES EVERYTHING

1. Do you agree with the premise that the frustrations with life come when we are trying to live out of alignment with our design? Why or why not? Where might you be feeling out of alignment right now?
2. Have you experienced the frustration of the Two-Way Mirror of Meaning, where you look to other people for clarity on your identity and purpose only to have them give you counsel and wisdom that is reflective of them and their purpose?
3. When in your life have you been the most full of joy, satisfaction, and peace? Do you agree that it was because in that season you were operating out of a place of truth and authenticity to who you were designed to be? Why or why not?

ACTION STEP

This week, pay attention to moments in your day when you feel out of alignment with the way you were designed to be. Write down where you were, who you were with, and what you were doing.

CHAPTER 2: THE INVISIBLE FORCE HOLDING YOU BACK

1. Where in your life do you feel conformity's pull the strongest? Consider the six core areas of life: your work, time, finances, relationships, health, and spirituality.
2. What have been some of the small (or large) decisions that you've abdicated along the way that got you to where you are now? What assumptions have you made about the way "life is supposed to be"? Were there any people you were trying to please along the way?
3. This chapter listed a few rebels in history who changed the world for the better. Can you think of some others who would fit that description whom you admire or look up to? In what area of life did they push back against conformity?

ACTION STEP

Pick one of the six core areas of life (work, time, finances, relationships, health, and spirituality) to focus on. Write down a list of your own assumptions or "outsourced" decisions that you've made in this area up to this point in your life.

CHAPTER 3: DREAMING IS THE MOST REBELLIOUS THING YOU COULD DO

1. What did you dream about when you were in high school or college? What about when you were first married or had kids of your own? Just take thirty seconds to think back and name one or two dreams that you had when you were younger.
2. Have you experienced a moment in your life where someone either explicitly or implicitly told you that it is foolish to dream and that you should be "realistic"? Did that cause you to stop dreaming? Why or why not?
3. Have you chased a dream that died and found yourself at the Identity Crisis Intersection? If so, describe what that felt like and what you chose to do next.

ACTION STEP

This week, carve out some time (at least an hour) and complete the fifty dreams exercise as outlined in chapter three. Take note of what surprised you the most from going through this process.

CHAPTER 4: THE BEST YEARS OF YOUR LIFE FRAMEWORK

1. Do you agree with the statement that "without a vision, your life is empty or void"? Why or why not?
2. Where in your life do you feel like you have the most clarity around your vision? What area of your life has the least clarity of vision?
3. Have you ever created a blueprint or vision for your life? If not, why? If so, what is working and what is not working with your vision?

ACTION STEP

Take about an hour to journal out your response to the best three years of your life exercise in chapter four including outlining your ideal day.

CHAPTER 5: REPROGRAM YOUR MIND WITH THE INNER STORY AUDIT

1. Do you agree with the premise that "we become what we think about"? Why or why not?
2. Have you experienced a time where you heard that "still, small voice" of intuition in your mind and acted on it? If so, what were the results?
3. Which of these five common negative mental scripts have you fallen prey to before?
   - "I'm not smart enough."
   - "It's too late to try something new."
   - "If I ________, this is what is going to happen."
   - "I don't have enough resources/money/connections/time."
   - "If I do ________, people will judge me."

ACTION STEP

Spend twenty minutes this week taking the Inner Story Audit as outlined in chapter five. If you feel comfortable, share the results with a trusted friend or family member.

CHAPTER 6: THE LIFE CHANGE FORMULA: BELIEVE, THINK, FEEL, DO

1. When have you seen this formula play out where you changed your beliefs, which ultimately led to different actions and results in your life?
2. How do you currently like to prime your day in the mornings? What elements of your morning routine (if you have one) make the biggest impact on how you feel throughout the day?
3. Do you have any "stones of remembrance" in your life (vision boards, dream journals, powerful quotes) that are set up near you for moments when you get discouraged? If so, what has been the most impactful for you?

ACTION STEP

Take twenty minutes this week to create your own "virtual board of advisors" as outlined in chapter six and then visualize your first "meeting" with them as you present a challenge or situation you are dealing with. Finally, write down your best next step to making your dream a reality.

CHAPTER 7: THE FINAL HURDLES TO LIVING THE REBEL LIFESTYLE

1. Where in your life have you let the illusion of perfectionism and the fear of things being messy get in the way of pursuing your goals and dreams?
2. Jon Gordon says, "If you love the process you will love what the process produces." Have you seen that to be true in your life? Why or why not?
3. Where in your life have you found yourself trying to live up to someone else's standards or caring too much about what other people think? How did that make you feel?

ACTION STEP

This week, take an hour to sit down and create (with your spouse if married) your own set of personal/family values based on the two key questions outlined in chapter seven.

CHAPTER 8: THE SURPRISINGLY SIMPLE WAY TO FIND YOUR LIFE'S PURPOSE

1. If you were to be asked "Who are you? And why are you here?" How would you answer those questions?
2. Do you agree with the statement that "your identity precedes your destiny"? Why or why not?
3. The premise of this chapter is that "once you know who you are, what you care about, what dreams light you up, and you begin to live out those dreams and desires, what flows out of living that freely in service of others is your purpose." Where have you seen that to be true in yourself or someone else?

ACTION STEP

Draw out a version of the Life Purpose Matrix as illustrated in chapter eight and begin to plot out some of the key tasks and pursuits in your life among the four quadrants. See what ends up in the top right Life Purpose quadrant.

ACKNOWLEDGMENTS

Writing this book has been one of the most life-giving and inspiring experiences of my life. As they say, "You write the book you most need to read." That has certainly been true for me with this one. But this book would not exist if it weren't for a handful of wonderful and important people in my life.

First, I'd like to thank all the readers of my first book, *How to Get Paid for What You Know*. If it weren't for so many of you buying, reading, and sharing that book, I would never have had the opportunity to sign a second book deal with my publisher.

To Jon Gordon, this book wouldn't exist without you. Back in February of 2023, Jon was kind enough to sit down with me for six hours and press me on what my next book would be about. We went around and around unpacking all I could teach and what my life story was. Then at one moment, Jon said something that resonated deeply with me: "Graham, you're a rebel! You've always been one. That's your story, and why you've been so successful." In that moment I knew we were on to something as he gave language to what I have always felt in my heart. I care deeply about doing business and life my way, and it has served me and my family well. Thank you, Jon, for sticking with me that day and fighting for the breakthrough that became this book. You've been a huge encouragement and mentor to me and I am forever grateful.

To my wife, Shay (a rebel in your own right), thank you for believing in me and this book. Thank you also for reading early drafts of the outline and chapters and helping me clarify the message of this book!

To my parents, Mike and Maria, for reading, reviewing, and giving feedback on every word of the original manuscript. Your support and enthusiasm have meant so much to me!

To Stephanie Lee, thank you for early brainstorming sessions as I fleshed out the framework and the organization of this material before sitting down to actually write it.

To all my coaches and mentors throughout the years who I either borrowed from or was indirectly influenced by, including Rory Vaden, Mike Zeller, Julia Woods, Rich Litvin, Cliff Ravenscraft, and Jordan Raynor. Thank you for your collective genius and for the work you do in the world.

To Matt Holt and the team at BenBella for believing in me and greenlighting book number two. This one is going to change so many lives!

To Katie Dickman for taking my words and making them better. I'm grateful for such a thorough and thoughtful editor.

And finally, thank you to Jesus (the ultimate Rebel) for being my savior, my guide, and my friend.

ABOUT THE AUTHOR

Photo by Stacey Poterson

Graham Cochrane is a seven-figure entrepreneur, TEDx and keynote speaker, bestselling author, and host of *The Graham Cochrane Show*, a top 0.5 percent ranked podcast globally, where each week he helps high performers create more money, margin, and meaning in their lives. With over fourteen years of online coaching and content experience, seven hundred thousand YouTube subscribers across his channels, and having built multiple seven-figure businesses that require less than five hours of work per week to run, Graham is a leading voice and coach in the life-giving business movement. His insights have been regularly featured in national media outlets like *Forbes*, CNBC, and *Business Insider*. He lives in Tampa, Florida, with his wife, Shay, and daughters, Chloe and Vera.

To learn more or book Graham to speak at your next event, please visit GrahamCochrane.com.

Follow Graham on Instagram @thegrahamcochrane.

TRANSFORM YOUR LIFE IN THE NEXT 30 DAYS

Ready to take what you've learned in this book and kickstart your Rebel Journey in the next 30 days? Then I have a bonus gift for you!

Inside the *30-Day Rebel Challenge* you'll discover:

- **A 4-week step by step plan to discover your true identity and step into your life's purpose**
- **Daily encouraging emails filled with helpful resources, exercises, and motivation to keep moving on your Rebel Journey**
- **Virtual coaching from me inside your inbox each day to help you not just read the book, but *live* the book so you can transform your life!**

Go to GrahamCochrane.com/rebelbonus to get started.